# AUGUSTINE OF HIPPO

# AUGUSTINE OF HIPPO

## *A Life*

Henry Chadwick

**OXFORD**
UNIVERSITY PRESS

# OXFORD
## UNIVERSITY PRESS

Great Clarendon Street, Oxford OX2 6DP

Oxford University Press is a department of the University of Oxford.
It furthers the University's objective of excellence in research, scholarship,
and education by publishing worldwide in

Oxford New York

Auckland Cape Town Dar es Salaam Hong Kong Karachi
Kuala Lumpur Madrid Melbourne Mexico City Nairobi
New Delhi Shanghai Taipei Toronto

With offices in

Argentina Austria Brazil Chile Czech Republic France Greece
Guatemala Hungary Italy Japan Poland Portugal Singapore
South Korea Switzerland Thailand Turkey Ukraine Vietnam

Oxford is a registered trade mark of Oxford University Press
in the UK and in certain other countries

Published in the United States
by Oxford University Press Inc., New York

British Library Cataloguing in Publication Data
Data available

Library of Congress Cataloging in Publication Data
Data available

Typeset by SPI Publisher Services, Pondicherry, India
Printed in Great Britain
on acid-free paper by
Clays Ltd., St Ives plc

ISBN 978-0-19-956830-7

1 3 5 7 9 10 8 6 4 2

For
JULIET

# FOREWORD

HENRY CHADWICK was the unsurpassed expositor, in our
times, of the thought of the Early Christians and of their
pagan contemporaries. He was also a translator of rare felicity.
He showed his talent first in an unsurpassed translation of the
answer of the Christian Origen to the pagan Celsus: the great
*Contra Celsum*—*Against Celsus*—written in around AD 248. To
read this translation, along with its indispensable footnotes, is
to hear again a very ancient Christianity in graceful dialogue
with the pagan world.[1] His translation of the *Confessions* of Saint
Augustine is a masterpiece provoked by a masterpiece.[2] It is
the work of a scholar who had explored the world-view of
the Neoplatonists which Augustine had absorbed. This world-
view implied an image of man, of mental and physical processes,
and of the universe that was thrillingly different from our own.
Like a star-filled sky, this world (and not a modern universe)
stood behind and above Augustine. Chadwick's translation makes
sure that we look up to see those incandescent stars, by which
Augustine steered his course as a thinker and as a religious writer.

As a result, in Chadwick's translation of the *Confessions* the
metaphysical passion of Augustine is enabled to shine through in
limpid English. Each phrase of the translation is carefully chosen
(and frequently justified in pertinent footnotes) by a past master

---

[1] H. Chadwick, *Origen: Contra Celsum* (Cambridge University Press, 1965).
[2] H. Chadwick, *Saint Augustine: Confessions* (Oxford University Press, 1991).

of Early Christian and Platonic thought. The result is a translation of rare beauty and precision which leads us gently but firmly away from the popular image of an Augustine wrapped in sin and sex and brings us instead the joy and crackle of an intellectual of the fourth century AD.

But beyond all this, Henry Chadwick was an intellectual narrator of magnetic power. He knew how to talk us through the life and thought of awesomely engaged and complex thinkers of the distant past with the skill of a great raconteur. This, perhaps, is not surprising. He was a man who loved music. Like his fellow-giant in the study of the Early Christian world, Henri-Irénée Marrou, he would have willingly numbered himself among those whom Augustine (who knew all too well the pull of music at the base of his own heart) described as persons 'who count themselves miserable when music is lacking to their lives' (*De libero arbitrio* 2. 13. 35).

Chadwick knew why he loved music:

Great music makes imperious demands ... It requires the listener to apply his attention even to familiar music as if he were hearing it for the first time and were continually wondering where the music will go next.[3]

It is precisely this thrill which Chadwick imparts to his intellectual profiles of the great thinkers and the great problems of the Early Christian world. He knew how to convey thought in motion. No one could seize with greater clarity and firmness the 'nerve centres' of entire systems of thought and of entire theological alignments. But he never froze these systems as static

---

[3] H. Chadwick, 'Why Music in Church?', *Tradition and Exploration. Collected Papers on Theology and the Church* (Norwich: Canterbury Press, 1994), 203–16, at 204.

structures. On the contrary, Chadwick always followed through, with a musician's sense of movement, the headlong logic of ideas, and the way by which these central propositions worked themselves out 'in real time', in the minds of individual thinkers and in the heat of long drawn out controversies. He did this for all the great minds and for all the major conflicts of the Christian Church: Origen, Augustine, and Boethius; the Arian and the Christological controversies, from the council of Nicaea (325) to the council of Chalcedon (451) and beyond; and, more slowly and saddest of all, he followed the growing rift between the eastern and the western churches from early times to the fall of Constantinople in 1453.

This book enables us to appreciate, at its height, Chadwick's gift as a riveting intellectual narrator. The manuscript of the book was discovered among his papers. It was the draft of a life of Augustine written in 1981 for the Past Masters series of Oxford University Press, which was eventually replaced by a different, shorter text (1986). That masterpiece of condensation is now available (with an updated bibliography) as *Augustine: A Very Short Introduction* in what is known (with appropriate brevity) as the Oxford VSI series (2001). The longer account printed here enables us to savour to the full (as those shorter texts do not) the artistry of Chadwick. We can see him at work recapturing the full texture of Augustine's life and thought.

For of one thing about Augustine Chadwick was certain. He was a man endowed with a rare capacity to see 'in the limited circumstances of his life and times an element of the universal'. He was a man whose thought emerged from the rough texture of real life. And Chadwick, in all his work, had an unfailing sense of life. He had a gift for seizing on a vivid piece of evidence (hidden like a bright coin in the dust of so many volumes of the *Patrologia Latina*) which gave life and wit to an entire past age.

Reading this book, we are in no doubt that we are in a world not like our own. Slaves cost the equivalent of three carthorses. The mentally defective served as toys of the rich. A spike in interest rates sparked a wave of violence which swept the country-side. There are bishops in abundance. But they are not like our bishops—or so we sincerely hope. The system of promotion by seniority to the position of Primate of Numidia (roughly, modern Algeria) produced 'two bishops of extreme senectitude' locked in irresoluble conflict. One such grumpy old man, by the way, had accused Augustine of sending a love spell to a noble lady, to help her in her adultery by calming down a jealous husband. Another bishop took on the job so as to use the funds of the church 'as a device for concealing a vast tax fiddle'. In a small Numidian agro-town, one bishop was found lying on an ash heap, seriously wounded (the work of his ecclesiastical opponents) by a peasant who had gone to piss against the wall, while his wife modestly kept her distance. But it was also an Africa where men came down to the hills to meet their bishop:

What do you want?
To know the glory of God (*EP* 134. 22).

This is a book about Augustine which has the tang of life. But these details are far more than local colour. They are there for a purpose. Chadwick places each one of them with care along the line of his exposition of Augustine's thought. They are the real life experiences of a real world which provoked this thought, which determined the tone in which this thought was communicated, and which pushed Augustine's mind ever further forward, towards vast intellectual projects and into resonant controversies.

Hence a quality of the book which I (not being a musician) would describe on the humble analogy of an adventure playground. It is a book full of thrills. In analysing Augustine's theory of knowledge, we begin gently. Knowledge is conveyed by signs. Some signs are ambiguous. They require knowledge of the circumstances and the cultural patterns in which they are used, even, at times, of the body-language of the speaker. When an African farmer says *abundat*—'He has a fine crop'— he means the opposite: he has a fine crop of worries—the poor man is bankrupt. It is a charming detail. But then, whoosh! Within a page we are hurtling down a slide. Vertiginous issues lay hidden behind these homely anecdotes. Given the arbitrariness, the deliberate ambiguity and the cultural determination of human signs, what then ensures the communication of mind to mind? Now we are racing at full speed down our slide.

Education presupposes theology, a God-given capacity 'for communion of minds beyond the merely external uses of sounds and symbolic acts'. And the thrill continues. Language alone cannot convey all thoughts. A vast reserve of inexpressible thoughts gathers in the mind. Augustine points the way to the subconscious. But there is room for God-given signs—valid echoes of His own language, as He calls to human kind. And so we touch on the eucharist. Only a page further on we have reached the most illuminating exposition that a reader will ever find, in the English language, of the famous Augustinian distinction between *uti* and *frui* (between 'to use' and 'to enjoy')—a distinction central to Augustine's view of a Christian's relation to culture and society. An exposition which began with the glum irony of an African farmer has taken us, in a few pages only, about as deep as anyone can go.

Hence the remarkable structure of the book. Issues that arise from real life do not necessarily follow the straight lines laid down for the abstract exposition of systems of thought. To follow the thought of Augustine, in this book, is to follow the grain of a very complex piece of wood. Great works which are usually placed first in standard expositions of Augustinian thought often appear in this book where we would least expect them to appear. We have to wait until we reach over halfway through this book to meet the *Confessions*. For, with extreme care, Chadwick delineates the problems which led up to the writing of the *Confessions*—the 'ascending foothills and soaring ridges' which rose towards that high peak.

Nor do the great issues of Augustinian theology appear where we usually expect them. Thus, it is in the middle of a vivid evocation of the rambunctious quality of Augustine's Christian congregations in Hippo and Carthage that the issue of love and the working of God's grace first surfaces—roughly a third of the book before we reach the Pelagian Controversy, where such themes are usually discussed. But Chadwick places the issue exactly where it should be placed—in Augustine's long (and surprisingly generous) musings on the capacity of such unprepossessing human material as the average African Christian to be touched by the love of God and to experience conversions quite as amazing as his own—if that much less voluble.

Last but not least, Henry Chadwick was a churchman. Though he wrote with admirable detachment, he was never disengaged. The sharpness of thought and the humanity which he displayed in all his work were nourished by the sense of living in a community whose traditions reached back to the distant past. These traditions could be a source of life and comfort to millions. They could also come, over the centuries, to pass down their fair share of toxic waste. In such a situation, history mattered. It was Chadwick's constant concern to reach back into that past. He sought to seize the thought and practice of the Church, as it changed over the centuries. Only by such careful study was it possible to find a way, in modern times, towards a common language on which Christian communities, long divided, might reach agreement.[4] His work concentrated, by preference, both on Christian controversies and on controversial Christians. For on issues of such urgency as the divisions of Christians, there simply could not be too much scholarship; there could not be too much clear thinking; there could not be too much alert searching of the past. The alternative had been hatred, in the past, and, in the present age, mindless alienation and the clasping of petty differences as if they were precious, ancestral tokens of identity.

For Chadwick, the historian of the Christian Church had a serious task: 'division brings evils in its train—evils to which we become insensitive by habit. Patient listening can uncover deep and wide agreement concealed by the polemics of the past . . . '.[5] 'Patient listening' was Chadwick's greatest gift to his readers, on any subject on which he touched. And so was the clear moral sense, steeled as much by contemporary experience as by millennia of Christian history, which he developed in the course of that listening. Schism and lasting division was the work of human

[4] H. Chadwick, 'Ecumenical Stocktaking: Unfinished Business', *Tradition and Exploration. Collected Papers on Theology and the Church* (Norwich: Canterbury Press, 2004), 143–53, esp. at 144–5.

[5] H, Chadwick, *East and West. The Making of a Rift in the Church. From Apostolic Times to the Council of Florence* (Oxford University Press, 2003), 275.

agents. The history of the Christian churches had its fair share of human agents gone wrong. There had been bullies, loudmouths, inflexible ideologues, sloppy thinkers, and obfuscators. Like the Lord High Executioner in the *Mikado*, Henry Chadwick had them on his list. Some of them appear in his works almost as comic relief. My favourite is Pope Symmachus, a contemporary of Boethius in the early sixth century. Blocked by the local aristocracy and tarnished by a widely proclaimed relationship with a courtesan called Conditaria—Spice Girl—'His policy was to make no concessions in theology or otherwise, and to assert Rome's universal jurisdiction with unrelenting fortissimo.'[6]

But, of course, the matter was more serious. The greatest minds might often be the most tragically wrong. On this issue Chadwick never flinched. He knew 'source pollution' of the Christian environment when he saw it. As a result, for all the human sympathy with which he followed the twists and turns of Augustine's life and thought, Augustine was not immune from his strictures. Chadwick says it as it is. In linking sexuality to original sin, by arguing inflexibly from a widespread, romantic idealization of the total virginity of Christ and Mary, 'Augustine injected a powerful and toxic theme into medieval theology.'[7] In the present book, Augustine's obfuscation on the issue of sex and original sin is handled no more kindly. Augustine's expressions on this loaded topic 'could easily confirm suspicions that Augustine is being deliberately oracular'.

The last great controversy, between Augustine and the Pelagian Julian of Eclanum, on marriage, sex, and original sin, is vividly

---

[6] H. Chadwick, *Boethius: The Consolations of Music, Logic, Theology and Philosophy* (Oxford: Clarendon Press, 1981), 31.

[7] H. Chadwick, *Augustine*, Past Masters (Oxford University Press, 1986), 114.

named 'A storm of criticism: hell and sex'. And it is Julian, not Augustine, who is left in possession of the battlefield.

It is part of the greatness of Chadwick as an expositor of Christian thought that his sense of responsibility to the present, as a patient listener to the past, made him so magnificently even-handed as a judge. Augustine had overstepped himself, and with serious, unforeseen consequences for the future of western Christianity. But this did not make him a monster—just a human being, seen in the round in this book. As Chadwick concludes:

His misfortune was to be treated as a towering authority in the history of western Christianity in a way that he himself would have strongly deplored. . . . There are obvious points where his arguments and standpoints invite attack . . . At least it can be said that Augustine had a deep abhorrence of being treated as a person whom people wanted to follow without pondering his reasons.

Chadwick has enabled us to ponder these reasons and to make up our own minds. I think that it can also be said that Augustine has not let him down. A newly discovered sermon, which was unknown when Chadwick drafted this manuscript, catches Augustine, once again, just as Chadwick has led us to see him. At some time, perhaps around 403, he had to preach (almost certainly in Carthage) on an issue of exegesis which intimately affected the nature of the Christian community. When St Paul tells us (in Gal. 2: 11) that he had 'opposed St Peter to his face' on the issue of allowing Jewish practices within the church, was this public disagreement no more than a set-up dialogue—a bad cop, good cop exchange—designed to raise the consciousness of the congregation on this issue? Or had the two men been sincerely opposed to each other? Augustine himself felt strongly that it had been a real conflict, and that only mutual love and absence of ego on both sides had enabled it to be resolved. Under pressure to pontificate on an issue in which major contemporary intellectuals were involved (to say nothing of the reputation of the Apostles Peter and Paul) Augustine refused to do so:

We, who preach and write books . . . write while we make progress. We learn something new every day. We dictate at the same time as we explore. We speak as we are still knocking for understanding . . . I urge Your Charity [the congregation], on my behalf and in my own case, that you should not take any previous book or preaching of mine as Holy Scripture . . . If anyone criticizes me when I have said what is right, he does not do right. But I would be more angry by far with the one who praises me and takes what I have written as Gospel truth than the one who criticizes me unfairly.[8]

This is the Augustine which Henry Chadwick has given to us. We are deeply grateful for the gift.

PETER BROWN

*Princeton University*
*16 November 2008*

---

[8] Augustine, *Dolbeau Sermon* 10. 15. 347, ed. F. Dolbeau, *Vingt-six sermons au peuple d'Afrique* (Paris: Institut d'Études Augustiniennes, 1996), 55, cited in P. Brown, *Augustine of Hippo: A New Edition with an Epilogue* (Berkeley: University of California Press, 2000), 451, with commentary. I am less certain than I was at that time as to the exact date and place of this sermon.

# ACKNOWLEDGEMENTS

I AM indebted to Professor Gillian Clark and officers of the Oxford University Press, especially Tom Perridge and Leofranc Holford-Strevens, for their help in resurrecting this manuscript written by Henry Chadwick in 1981 and preparing it for publication.

M. E. CHADWICK

# CONTENTS

# ABBREVIATIONS

| | |
|---|---|
| AO | De anima et eius origine |
| B | De baptismo |
| BC | De bono coniugali |
| BV | De beata vita |
| C | Confessiones |
| CD | De civitate Dei |
| CE | De consensu evangelistarum |
| CEP | Contra epistulam Parmeniani |
| CG | De correptione et gratia |
| CLP | Contra litteras Petiliani |
| CR | De catechizandis rudibus |
| DA | De duabus animabus |
| DP | De dono perseverantiae |
| DQ | De diversis quaestionibus LXXXIII |
| DS | De diversis quaestionibus ad Simplicianum |
| E | Epistolae |
| EJ | Tractatus in epistolam Johannis ad Parthos |
| EP | Enarrationes in Psalmos |
| F | Contra Faustum Manichaeum |
| FO | De fide et operibus |
| G | Epistolae ad Galatas expositio |
| GC | De gratia Christi |
| GL | De Genesi ad litteram |
| IIepPel | Contra duas epistolas Pelagianorum |
| J | Contra Julianum |
| LA | De libero arbitrio |
| M | De mendacio |
| ME | De moribus ecclesiae catholicae et de moribus Manichaeorum |
| NC | De nuptiis et concupiscentia |
| O | De ordine |
| OI | Opus imperfectum contra Julianum |

| | |
|---|---|
| *OM* | *De opere monachorum* |
| *PM* | *De peccatorum meritis* |
| *QA* | *De quantitate animae* |
| *QH* | *Quaestiones in Heptateuchum* |
| *R* | *Retractationes* |
| *S* | *Sermones (SDen* = Denis's collection, *SFr* = Frangipane collection; both in Morin's volume, 1930) |
| *Solil.* | *Soliloquia* |
| *T* | *De trinitate* |
| *TJ* | *Tractatus in Johannis Evangelium* |
| *U* | *De unitate Ecclesiae (Epistola ad Catholicos)* |
| *UC* | *De utilitate credendi* |
| *VR* | *De vera religione* |

# I

# A PERSONAL QUEST

AUGUSTINE felt the cold. He is one of the few men of antiquity about whom we know a great deal of personal detail of this and a more serious kind.

No figure of the ancient world is more accessible to us. But we go to him for more than the vivid detail. He has a special place in the history of Christianity in the West, and through that place has left a permanent mark on the general consciousness of humanity. Augustine saw in the limited circumstances of his life and times an element of the universal, a clue to the very nature and destiny of man, a glimpse of what God intends for all of a fallen race. Thereby he became a thinker and analyst of the human condition with an extraordinary sense of the glory and the misery of man. Just because he looms so large in the story of Christianity and of the making of the European mind, it is never easy to achieve sufficient distance and detachment to see him in the round. His culture and training were initially more literary than philosophical, and merely as a literary figure he must rank as one of the most remarkable writers of his age. When he tells a story, its dramatic force is given the maximum effect by consummate artistry, with an exact eye for the differing motives of human character, but above all by the manifest affection that he feels towards frail mortals whose actions he thinks far from a model of conduct. His autobiographical *Confessions* contain numerous examples of this rare narrative gift where he is visibly acting out his own maxim 'Hate the sin, love the sinner' (*QA* 34. 78, S 4. 20). 'We are all human; let us hate, not one another, but errors and lies.' Without illusions about himself, he draws his readers into his personal quest for happiness as he feels himself driven to believe that there is nothing to keep the soul from starvation other than truth, beauty, and goodness; and they can be reached only by love, a purified and sublimated love, the beginning, middle, and end of all things.

Feeling—'the heart'—lies at the centre of whatever it is which impels a person on his way. Augustine is fascinated by the desires and ambitions which pull people's lives in this direction or that. He sees that a man's character is not described accurately by a list of epithets of his virtues or weaknesses, but rather by an examination of what he wants to achieve as shown by his actions. If you want to understand the values of a society, look at (*a*) its criminal code, (*b*) what it spends its money on.

Augustine cannot be understood at all if he is treated as some timeless figure out of relation to his age. His early boyhood coincides with the brief reign of the emperor Julian. The long conflict between a confident and conquering Christianity capturing Roman society and a fierce pagan counterattack forms the backcloth of much that he writes. By the time he is 21 years old, in 375, the first thrust of barbarian immigration into the Roman empire has occurred, casting a long shadow. His is the age of Alaric's Visigoths and their astounding sack of Rome in 410; of the unstoppable impetus that carries the Vandals from way out beyond the Rhine through Gaul and Spain until in 429 they cross the Straits of Gibraltar to occupy the western provinces of

Roman North Africa and to set up a pirate kingdom at Carthage. Augustine's death on 30 August 430 occurs during the Vandal siege of his city of Hippo (on the Algerian coast at modern Annaba or Bône) before the final collapse of the perimeter defences.

To the extent that some large proportion of society had ceased to believe in the old polytheism and adopted a general scepticism and materialism, it is fair to describe Augustine's age as 'decadent'; at least that is what he himself would have been happy to think. But in other respects his age has no more decadence than any other generation. The intellectual climate of his time is dominated in philosophy by the modern Platonism taught by Plotinus at Rome in the middle years of the third century AD. At a crucial stage of his quest this Neoplatonic philosophy came to have a permanent lodging in his mind.

By his educated contemporaries Augustine is esteemed as an exceptionally gifted man, but is not treated as a superhuman prodigy. An important element in whatever it is in him that is 'greatness' lies in an ability to articulate what the most alert people of his time were taking for granted even if (except for his senior contemporary Jerome) they could not have expressed themselves so eloquently. But he also articulated a belief about the nature of man which was divisive then and has remained so since. Augustine's readers then and now either find themselves Augustinians, though they may not have realized it previously, or feel him to be a formidably dark pessimist portraying a Kafka-like world that is unwelcome.

Augustine's life can be written on a miniature scale only by leaving much out. To tell all would be to end with a book the size of the brilliant and most indispensable of his biographies written by Le Nain de Tillemont (2nd edn. Paris, 1710), which runs to well over 1,000 pages. We are fortunate to possess a short biography by a contemporary and pupil, Possidius, who lived with him in the house at Hippo and was then put into the nearby town of Calama as bishop. Possidius' portrait is not of a great theologian (a side of Augustine that Possidius did not understand anyway) but of a heroic pastor of his people; Possidius has the merit of being an honest uninventive man, gasping with astonishment in the presence of personal greatness. His sketch perhaps provided an hour's discourse suitable for reading on the anniversary. He felt that the books and letters failed to convey the charismatic power of Augustine's personality as experienced by those who listened to him speaking.

The principal materials for Augustine's life are provided by his own writings. In addition to the narrative of his first 33 years in the *Confessions*, we have about 245 letters from his pen and many personal references in his treatises. About a thousand of his sermons survive and offer the biographer much exciting matter. Augustine is no egotist, but he thinks it unnecessary to exclude allusions to himself or recent events in discourses to his flock.

## The Making of a Professor

Augustine was born on 13 November 354.

He was not born with a silver spoon in his mouth. He was the child of small-town parents in Thagaste in the province of Numidia, now the large village of Souk-Ahras in Algeria not far from the Tunisian border. Thagaste lies in hilly country about 60 miles inland, south of Hippo on the coast. Hardly more than a few ruins of the bath-house now survive to remind the visitor of its Roman past (unlike Hippo of which much more has been found by the French archaeologists). Augustine's father Patrick sat on the town council and had the status of a *curialis*, in the late empire a hard-pressed class expected by the government to keep their local community going on their personal resources. Patrick owned but a few acres. His wife Monnica bore not only Augustine but also another son and two daughters. Their relative ages are never mentioned. Monnica came of a Christian family, but Patrick remained a pagan almost until the end of his life. Monnica was regular in giving alms for the poor, devoted to the honour of the martyrs of the African churches, and daily attendant at prayers in the local church morning and evening. Her constant devotions did not make her careless, and she avoided gossip. She was often influenced by her dream-life through which she felt that God guided her.

Both Augustine's parents are likely to have been of Berber stock, but Romanized and Latin-speaking. Numidian peasants of the fourth century spoke not Latin but Punic, inherited from the Phoenician settlers who came from Tyre and Sidon a millennium before to set up their trading station and maritime power at Carthage. In Hannibal they had once offered a frightening threat to Rome's ambitions to conquer the Mediterranean. As Romans settled in their North African provinces, many took Berber- or Punic-speaking wives. In the second century AD Apuleius, of Madauros near Thagaste, author of the *Golden Ass*, had a Punic-speaking wife. In Augustine's time the Punic-speakers retained a consciousness of their old Phoenician forefathers, and could manifest a lack of enthusiasm for the Roman administration of their country now established for over five centuries. Latin culture was a veneer; those who had it tended to despise those who had not. Augustine acquired a conversational knowledge of the patois, and never speaks of Punic language or culture with the least touch of scorn as the pagan Maximus of Madauros did. But his parents and nurses spoke to him in Latin, and education at the Thagaste school was principally in Latin language and literature, a subject which ancient men called 'grammar', taught by the *grammaticus*.

Augustine's schoolmaster, first at Thagaste, then until his sixteenth year at nearby Madauros, appears more notable for his skill with the cane than for offering a positive education. To the end of his days Augustine can hardly refer to the life of a schoolboy without recalling the misery of cruel floggings. He would not say it did him no good, for it was a training for the far greater troubles of adult life. But 'we learn better when freely trying to satisfy our curiosity than under fear or force' (*C* 1. 14. 23). Once he had been handed Virgil's *Aeneid*, his young mind was kindled to excitement by the exquisite poetry. His school also made him learn Greek, a language spoken by a substantial minority of the North African population with links to Sicily and South Italy where Greek was widespread. A mere hundred miles of sea separate Sicily from the North African coast. Augustine found Greek hard; the difficulty soured even the reading of Homer whose poetic power he admired. In later life he was generally inclined to protest too much his ignorance of Greek. After his schooldays he did not read classical Greek texts. But he could read the language with a dictionary. In 415 in the *City of God* he makes his own translation into Latin of a piece of Plotinus, and when writing *On the Trinity* he consulted works by acknowledged masters of the Greek East. Nevertheless a very Latin pride in the cultural world of Virgil, Cicero, Seneca, Terence, and his fellow-countryman Apuleius helped him to treat Greek theologians and philosophers as constructive helps rather than as authorities to be slavishly imitated. Aristotle first came before him in his early twenties when he was studying at Carthage. Except for Cicero's translation of the *Timaeus*, he seems to have read no Plato before he reached Milan in 384 aged 30. The standard education of the time was primarily in the art of persuasive oratory, including some logic. Looking back he realized he had come to think a fault in speech much graver than a failure in morality (*C* 1. 18. 29). Most of the philosophy he knew he taught himself by his reading. For the contemporary professional teachers of philosophy in the Latin West, he speaks in a letter of 386 in terms of utter contempt.

From his boyhood his health gave cause for anxiety. Aged about 7 he fell seriously ill with chest pains; when his death was expected he asked Monnica to arrange for his baptism. (As an infant he had been made a catechumen with the sign of the cross and salt on his tongue.) Recovery led to deferment. Throughout his life his health was precarious, and a series of bouts of sickness made him appear prematurely old in middle age. Although after he had become a bishop his burdens were far heavier, he nevertheless seems to have enjoyed better health under greater strain. The optimum degree of tension is not nil.

Patrick nursed ambitions for his clever son. Towards Patrick Augustine shows small sign of sympathy. The devout Monnica hoped to persuade Patrick to become a Christian; perhaps once faith had come, her often erring husband would be more faithful to her. In pagan households of the time the master of the house took it for granted that he had a right to sleep with his serving girls, and preachers did not find it easy to convince Christian congregations that this right should not be exercised (*S* 224. 3). Patrick was hot-tempered, but Monnica kept out of his way when he was cross, and so 'escaped the battering other wives receive'. Yet when serene, he was kind. Monnica herself felt it a harmonious relationship (*C* 9. 11. 28). They both realized that if finance could be found, an education at the metropolis at Carthage (by modern Tunis) could open the door to success in the great world. But when Augustine was 16, Patrick died, after being baptized during his last sickness. For Augustine a wild demoralized year followed while means were sought to enable him to continue his studies, a project in which he was eventually assisted by a wealthy landowner of Thagaste, Romanianus. (His name appears on an inscription dug up at Thagaste.) In the *Confessions* Augustine vividly describes how he stole pears from a nearby orchard not out of any wish for the fruit, which was of inferior quality, but because there is a pleasure in doing something forbidden. As he looked back on the incident, he felt himself to be repeating the experience of Adam in Genesis. The pears were accidental to the substance of his enjoyment which was simply the doing wrong; that made the story significant, not a mere adolescent prank of the most boring triviality. He went to Carthage with his mother's timely exhortation that he avoid fornication, above all adultery with another man's wife.

Carthage was 'a seething cauldron of shameful sex'. 'I was in love with being in love'. Augustine came to know the longing to discover love and, simultaneously, the destruction of both friendship and inward self-respect which results from egotistic seeking of sensual pleasure. Through the heat of adolescent calf-love, the incapacity of human nature for pure altruism began to impinge on his consciousness. His undergraduate prayer was 'Grant me chastity but not yet' (C 8. 7. 17). 'Under the sway of passion man is as uncontrollable as a flash flood or hot wax' (EP 57. 16–20).

Unlike Thagaste or Madauros, Carthage was part of the great world of high culture. Since the occupation of North Africa by Muslim Arabs, more than two centuries after Augustine's lifetime, a cultural and religious gulf has existed between the north and south sides of the Mediterranean lake. This was not at all the case three centuries before the Arabs when Augustine was at school. From Libya to Morocco prosperous provinces of the Roman empire exported grain, wine, and olive oil. Throughout the third century there had been a recession in trade; but prosperity returned in the fourth century and Carthaginian merchants of Augustine's acquaintance enjoyed a far-flung and lucrative trade as far as India. The standard of living was often at least as high as that in many parts of Italy. Augustine records his astonishment at finding in Italy well-to-do people without a bedroom to themselves, which Africans would take for granted (O 1. 3. 6). The ambition of rich citizens was to be 'buried in an expensive sarcophagus at a funeral attended by columns of slaves both male and female, and a procession of dependent clients' (S 102. 1. 2, 2. 3). Their villas were adorned with marble and rich mosaic (such as one may see in the Bardo Museum at Tunis). Carthage had a substantial concentration of sophisticated people of high Latin culture. High officials of the Roman administration there counted a poet or an orator or a civilized bishop a welcome guest at dinner. A century previously Carthage had had the first bishop to come from the senatorial class, Cyprian, martyred in 258 and the glory of the African churches. In Augustine's time his feast-day (14 September) was celebrated with dancing at his shrine by the harbour.

At Carthage in 373 the 19-year-old Augustine was required by the syllabus of study to read a text 'by a certain Cicero' (as he would ironically put it): the dialogue entitled *Hortensius* which medieval scribes failed to copy but which survives through over 100 quotations mainly in Augustine. The book, recommended for its fine style, had a moral content which Augustine, in his retrospect of a quarter of a century later, felt to have changed his life. Already he was by temperament a quiet and bookish person repelled by rowdy students. Here was Cicero telling him to be self-sufficient; to know there is no happiness in merely doing as one pleases (to be free but do wrong is merely the road to misery); to cultivate detachment from wealth and to practice solitude; to realize that if the aim is the highest contemplation and purification of one's immortal soul, one should not only eat and drink frugally but also live unmarried—for 'bodily pleasure is a distraction to the mind'; to admit that even oratory itself, the very door to worldly success, is not the greatest thing in life. The ultimate and dominant need is to find happiness. Men fail to find it, Cicero thought, because they seek the unobtainable or the harmful or the worthless. The dialogue concluded with the sombre reflection that the misery of man is a divine judgment: we are born to atone by punishment for sins in a higher life. Augustine was moved by these sentiments and disappointed only that Cicero's philosophical scepticism despaired of truth's attainability; 'he had no room for Christ'. Augustine also found himself divided in mind by the recommendation not to marry.

Already, aged 17, Augustine had come to keep house with a girl-friend of servile status. Augustine was never promiscuous— 'she was the only one and I was faithful to her'—but Monnica was never happy about the relationship. Augustine portrays himself as simply needing sex. The couple quickly had an initially unwanted but soon much-loved son to whom they gave the common African name Adeodatus or 'God's gift' (the Latin equivalent of the Greek Theodore). As a teenager Adeodatus showed acute abilities, but died aged about 18. Even in a pagan society it was more respectable to be legally married: it meant legitimacy and 'bona fama' (*Solil.* I. II. 10). The relation of concubinage was less respectable than legal marriage, but not considered publicly scandalous. Marriage with a girl of servile status was in any event illegal. The Church accepted such couples as being *de facto* married provided the relation remained monogamous; if so, they were not debarred from admission to the sacraments.

During his turbulent years Augustine's inheritance of faith became submerged by his sensual nature. When he first began studying at Carthage he had attended church services but mainly (so he felt in self-critical retrospect) to catch the eyes of pretty girls on the other side of the basilica. (African church custom segregated the sexes, keeping the laity standing while bishop and presbyters were seated.) He became fascinated by the theatre. None of his teachers commanded his respect and admiration, but he liked reading and found his way to important books. The spiritual stirrings occasioned by Cicero's *Hortensius* led him to pick up his Bible again. Quickly he put it down. The old Latin version of the Bible had none of the noble classical prose of, say, the Authorized (King James) Version or Luther's German Bible. It had been put together hurriedly in the second century, probably by the missionaries who brought Christianity to North Africa. Especially in the Old Testament the version abounds in vulgar idiom and gross literalism. It defies the rules acknowledged by Cicero or Caesar. Its deficiencies are such that Jerome would soon produce a drastically corrected version which we now call the Vulgate or 'generally received' translation, which it very gradually came to be, but not until after much conservative opposition of which, as a bishop, Augustine himself was in part the mouthpiece. The young Augustine was appalled by the humble vulgarity of the old version, and had no motivation to press beyond form to content. As a guide for life's decisions he turned for a few years to astrology.

The need to earn bread for his widowed mother and family took Augustine back to Thagaste for a year or so, where he opened a school of grammar and rhetoric. At this time the death of a close friend caused him profound depression; for much of his life the fear of losing friends by death haunted him. Then the municipal chair of rhetoric at Carthage fell vacant, a post carrying a basic salary provided by the government, further supplemented by the students' fees. Such appointments much depended on influence. Perhaps through Romanianus Augustine got the job. Although far too many of the students were given to acts of mindless vandalism, which caused him gloom, his lectures on Cicero's *Rhetorica* were profitable at least to a handful of grateful pupils. We hear accidentally of one who a few years later had to lecture on Cicero himself, and experienced agonies of anxiety at his own professional inadequacy until, in a dream, Augustine explained it all. One of his best pupils was a law student from Thagaste, Alypius, who became a lifelong friend. Augustine in his spare time also studied the law.

## Mani

At Carthage both Augustine and Alypius, and through them others, were drawn into the orbit of the Manichees, a half-secret theosophical society originating in Mesopotamia with Mani (216–76). Mani taught a fusion of religious elements drawn from Zoroastrianism, Buddhism, and gnostic Christian sects, by which he aspired to transcend regional tribalism in religion and to construct a world-faith for all.

The problem of evil is central in Manichaeism. Mani explained evil by a myth of pre-cosmic conflict between equal powers of light and darkness, a theme elaborated with fantastic imagination and with elements of solar and lunar cult. He believed that fragments of the divine light captured by the evil powers of darkness have become imprisoned in the bodies of men and beasts, which his rites and doctrines are designed to liberate. In redemption God is therefore recovering lost bits of himself. Mani entitled himself 'apostle of Jesus Christ', and claimed to be the Paraclete whom Jesus had promised, supplementing and correcting orthodox Christians with a final revelation about the meaning of the sacred books. Like most gnostics, Mani rejected the Old Testament as including too many cruel and unedifying stories to be deemed God's word. He accepted a shorter New Testament purged of 'interpolations' falsely portraying Christianity as a fulfilment and continuation of the Old Testament. The 'interpolations' include the infancy narratives in Matthew and Luke (whose genealogies are so divergent), narratives presupposing that the crucifixion of the Son of God could be a physical reality (since he really had no body like ours at all), and any other texts at variance with Manichee dogma. But Pauline letters, and especially Romans 8, were highly valued. The principle and source of evil is called Hylé, the Greek word for matter; but Mani's god of light is not actually non-physical; he is a vital presence permeating plant and animal life.

Mani's adherents were divided into two grades, Elect and Hearers. The Elect were celibate; from them Manichee clergy were recruited. They lived on a vegetarian diet supplied and cooked for them by Hearers, especially eating light-coloured fruits like melons and cucumbers. Lest they be guilty of 'murder', the Elect would not pick the fruit themselves. They were not allowed to till the soil, but could make a living e.g. by usury, which involved no ritual pollution. Hearers were allowed to marry, till the soil, and eat meat. No Manichee was allowed wine, 'a diabolical poison'. Married Hearers were allowed conjugal intercourse but ought to practice contraception or even abortion to avoid begetting children, by which process further imprisonment of the divine light takes place. Manichees observed the 'safe period' of the menstrual cycle.

The Manichee mission spread fast. It provoked hostility both in Persia, where Mani himself suffered execution, and in the Roman empire, where the emperor Diocletian thought it a corrupt occultism exported into his realm by a hostile Persian government to corrode his subjects. Fourth-century Manichees lived so as not to attract public notice. Shortly after Augustine left Carthage for Italy, the circle was severely harassed by the proconsul of Africa.

Mani presented his bizarre mythology as a rational, scientific knowledge contrasted with the mere faith asked by the Church. Augustine was attracted and, at the price of distressing Monnica, became a Hearer for ten years associated with the Manichee group in Carthage, being by his own account a very zealous member. Monnica would not have him in her house for a time; but a wise bishop whom she consulted reassured her: 'It cannot be that the son of these tears will be lost' (*C* 3. 12. 21). He did not think of Manichee adherence as a break with Christ, but only with the Church of which he was highly critical. After his conversion to Catholic Christianity a Manichee reader of the *Confessions* named Secundinus told him he had never really assimilated the great truths; and probably his mind always had mental reservations about some of the mythological clap-trap. Later his Pelagian critics would say he had assimilated Mani like an incurable virus. One grand question from Mani certainly remained to worry him: Whence comes evil? Mani answered by saying divine power is limited; and that answer came to seem dissatisfying.

In his twenties at Carthage Augustine studied mathematics, geometry, and music. He tried to interpret what he learnt from Manichee myths about the divine light being imprisoned in darkness, with the help of philosophical pantheism. He wrote an essay on the beauty of the pantheistic understanding of the world entitled 'On Beauty and on what is fitting' (that is, on what has its due place in the proportion of things). He dedicated this to a successful philosophical orator at Rome, Hierius, held to be of taste and reputation, whose support he clearly hoped to enlist. His eye was already on the patrons of Rome. Although the book was lost from his library at the time he wrote the *Confessions*, its general theme is one he restates several times in writings after his conversion. But Augustine the Manichee experiments with explanations of evil in Stoic and Neopythagorean language, using quasi-philosophical jargon which in the retrospect of the *Confessions* Augustine will judge mumbo-jumbo, certainly the inventions of a mind far distant from orthodox Christianity.

Gradually gnawing doubts grew about the reconciliation of Mani and science. In Manichee belief about sun and moon, eclipses needed an explanation, and Augustine was troubled that the Manichee account was incompatible with the best natural science. He attended disputations in Carthage, where a Catholic layman named Elpidius formulated objections to which the Manichee replies seemed weak. Among Manichee leaders in Africa a high reputation was enjoyed by Faustus of Milev (modern Mila), and Augustine was assured that after hearing Faustus all his doubts would be resolved. Faustus came and brought only disillusion. Moreover, Augustine had come to have a few moral qualms. The Manichees delighted to notice every sexual lapse among the Catholic community and contrasted this with their own rigorous ideals. But a suspicion that private lives were at variance with the austere façade was confirmed when a young virgin who kept house for one of the Elect became pregnant. Inward withdrawal from Manichaeism was taking place during 383 when he moved from Carthage to a chair in Rome where both pay and prestige were higher and, above all, the students were not turbulent. He soon found, however, that they were not honest about paying their dues. At Rome, where Alypius preceded him, he found his way to the Manichee community, one of whom nursed him through a dangerous illness. He was favourably struck by an ascetic community which one Manichee, unsuccessfully, tried to establish in his house at Rome. Through the Manichees of Rome he won an introduction to, and the potent patronage of, the mighty pagan aristocrat Symmachus, city prefect and ardent defender of pagan cult against the attacks of Ambrose bishop of Milan.

## Milan

Through Symmachus' influence, Augustine in the autumn of 384 became professor of rhetoric at Milan, residence of the emperor Valentinian II and his powerful mother Justina, and the centre of real power. At Milan on 1 January 385 he had the honour of giving a panegyric on the emperor at the consular inauguration of a Frankish army general. His provincial accent (Africans did not distinguish long and short vowels) caused wry comment, but he did well enough to have hopes of being nominated a provincial governor. One of the first people he called upon at Milan was Ambrose who received him most kindly.

Ambrose until 374 had been the governor of the province of Liguria, but by popular demand was suddenly pressed into being bishop of Milan. A highly cultivated person, he had fluent Greek as well as Latin and drew not only on Greek theologians for his sermons but also on the modern Platonists, Plotinus and Porphyry. Augustine went to hear him preach out of regard for his oratory, but soon found the content gripped him. The spiritual reading of the Old Testament eliminated old Manichee objections, and also made free use of the language of Neoplatonic mysticism. Neoplatonic texts were studied by a Christian reading-group of educated laity, led by a wise old man named Simplician. (He may have been a presbyter; in 397 he succeeded Ambrose as bishop.) The Plato circle was supported by a distinguished senator Manlius Theodorus, whose patronage Augustine was glad to enjoy, though much later he regretted some compromise that the senator had felt impelled to make with pagan custom. Augustine passed from Manichaeism into scepticism, a mood which took him back to Cicero's philosophical dialogues. Elegant and civilized scepticism was at that time characteristic of many well-educated Romans.

The wealthy aristocracy initially felt Christianity to be embarrassingly un-Roman; but from about 350, by a gradual process lasting 150 years, they were converted. First the women came, then the men. They enriched churches by their gifts of mosaic and marble decoration or helped to build exquisite basilicas like Santa Sabina at Rome, erected on the Aventine during the last decade of Augustine's life, with finely decorated doors showing Biblical scenes, still to be seen. Virgil's Sibylline prophecy of an imperial child coming to introduce a golden age came to be widely interpreted of Jesus—a prophecy which Augustine felt to resemble that of Caiaphas in St John's Gospel who did not realize what he was saying. (The mature Augustine, though happy to say divine revelation is not confined to the Biblical canon, is cool to the Sibyl, Hermes Trismegistus, Orpheus, and other oracular pretenders.)

Simplician quoted to Augustine a pagan Platonist who used to say that the prologue to St John's Gospel ought to be inscribed in letters of gold in churches. Augustine seems to have owed to Simplician the thought that everything in the prologue is entirely in Plato's spirit until 'The Word was made flesh', a declaration bringing the corrective of humility to the pride of man. Simplician told Augustine the story of Marius Victorinus, the most eminent orator-philosopher of fourth-century Rome who was also an African by birth. Several of Victorinus' writings survive.

A pagan drawn towards Christianity, Victorinus had translated some Plotinus and Porphyry into Latin and also studied the Bible. Inwardly he came to feel himself a Christian, or at least a strong admirer of Christ if not yet of the Church. He remained an unbaptized fellow-traveller until, suddenly, he was ashamed of being ashamed. He gave in his name for instruction preparatory for baptism, and declined the offer of the Roman clergy of a private ceremony to spare any blushes (something we often, they explained, arrange for prominent personages). The moral of Simplician's story was not lost on Augustine.

Meanwhile Augustine was joined at Milan by others from home—Alypius (still a loose Manichee adherent), Monnica herself, anxious to be close to him now her other children were grown up, and another clever friend from Carthage named Nebridius, a man with an inquiring mind especially in religion, who 'hated a short answer to a great question'. Very possibly they came as rival competitors for Augustine's religious allegiance as well as for the pleasure of his brilliant conversation and extraordinary genius for friendship. The *Confessions* presuppose a concentration of ambitious young Africans at Milan, explicable if one of the influential palace officials, with posts in his patronage, came from that part of the world and could be expected, in the manner of the times, to have a sense of regional patriotism. Alypius was on the make and obtained an introduction to a powerful senator on whom he frequently attended. Augustine too was consumed with ambition. Monnica shared his high hopes.

Monnica realized that to win the glittering prizes, her son needed a sound wife. No one at Milan was likely to arrange for Augustine to be offered a high post under the crown if his bed and board were shared by a Carthaginian concubine with a teenage son. By law he could not marry her, and the pagan pattern would have been to send her away. Monnica saw that Adeodatus' mother must go if her matchmaking for the sake of her son's career were to have a chance. To both Augustine and the girl the parting was extremely painful. He felt a long-lasting wound. She went vowing (perhaps as a devoted and baptized Christian) that she would never go with another man, a declaration Augustine could hardly have recorded if he knew things had later turned out otherwise. The couple were the victims of the Roman class system and its intense social pressures to maintain a rigid stratification and discourage social mobility. Augustine writes as if, for all his love for his mother, he resented the position into which she and the system forced him. It did not occur to anyone concerned that for a serving girl's sake he ought to forgo his ambitions. The modern reader of the *Confessions* must be outraged by Augustine's dismissal of his son's mother; but the indictment has to read that he was not other than a man of his time. And he was not yet a Christian. We do not learn what Romanianus thought; he had invested a lot of money in Augustine's future.

Roman society expected a marriage to be arranged by the parents, and for the girl to be 12 or 13, at the start of puberty. The bride that Monnica found for him still had a couple of years to go. Augustine found himself bereft, with no companion. To allay the pain left by the loss of his beloved, and perhaps out of not wholly suppressed anger against Monnica's goodhearted concern, he tried taking another concubine. Ovid would have thought it sound advice. But the wound of the parting merely festered, and he ended the new relationship in self-disgust. Quietly the project of a marriage also fell away. His friend Alypius was much against it.

After a furtive experience in early adolescence Alypius regarded the sexual act as repulsive and humiliating. The ideal of continence had been for him among the attractions of Manichaeism. He too was moving into a Ciceronian scepticism about the possibility of religious certitude. He put pressure on Augustine to remain a bachelor and to set up house with him, perhaps with some of their other African friends in Milan. Romanianus appeared in Milan on legal business, and declared himself glad to finance a community engaged in contemplative discussion away from the hubbub of the world, if that could be realized. For a period Augustine passed through much emotional stress. In December 384 in the streets of Milan he had been inwardly disturbed by a beggar blissfully happy with intoxication. The contrast between the poor man's shortlived but carefree happiness and his own malaise plunged him deeper into moral despair and metaphysical doubts, which now became a hammering crescendo at the door.

## Plato

Meanwhile Augustine's readings in the Platonists Plotinus and Porphyry in Latin translation, were convincing him that ultimate reality must be non-physical, a concept very different from that of Manichee light.

The Platonists argued that our experience of flux and successiveness is at a distance from higher reality which is unchanging. We long for satisfaction of our moral aspirations in a supreme Goodness, in derivation from which diverse earthly things are esteemed good, and for the satisfaction of our aesthetic sensibility in a supreme Beauty to which beautiful things on earth are signposts. Truth, beauty, and goodness are eternal, above time and space. That there are timeless unchanging truths is demonstrable from mathematics. It is always true that the cube of 3 is 27, but not that the horse is at the door. Change is bound up with the successiveness of time and with the transience of physical objects in space. The world is an ordered cosmos in which everything has its own level or grade of existence. The Good at the apex of all existence is free of all limitation from particularity, the fount of being, and the ultimate Monad or One, in contrast with the plurality and conflicting vanity of earthly things. As one descends the great chain of being, in which each effect is inferior to its cause, one also increases the limitations of physicality and therefore reduces the degree of both being and goodness. This conception explains 'evil' which is a defect of goodness rather than a positive force with an independent substantiality. At times, however, Platonists also speak of matter as the root of change and therefore of evil. They think of creation as a divine ordering of a pre-existent and in part recalcitrant matter.

The Platonists speak of the soul as fallen by an act of free choice and as needing purification by liberation from bodily ties and passions. The soul needs to recover its wings. It is an immaterial entity, immortal and eternal, whose true home is with the eternal verities transcending this world of change and becoming. The soul pre-exists the body but even now retains a fragmentary half-conscious memory of its heavenly home to which it seeks to return. By contemplation or quietism (*otium* is Augustine's word) one may seek to set one's prophetic soul free to ascend to the ecstatic, dreamlike experience of union with God and a beatific vision which is inexpressible happiness.

The Platonists strongly hold the providential ordering of the world, mainly on the basis of the unending orbits of the starry heavens above, the stars being for Plato 'visible gods', and the moral law within. The discomforts, inconveniences, and even disasters of human life are either the consequences of our mistaken choices or providence's painful way of reminding us that this material earth is not the realm of our ultimate destiny. If there are men about of evil will, a discerning observer will see that they commonly bring greater misery to themselves than to their victims. The Platonists see providence in the regularity of the natural order, the laws of nature, the annual recurrence of the seasons, the framework of the environment in which mankind is called to discover itself. They do not look for signs of providence in apparent breaks in the natural order. This cosmic harmony of things has an earthly counterpart in music, a science dependent on mathematical proportion which, according to Plato's *Timaeus*, has a hidden affinity with the structure of the soul.

Plotinus and his Neoplatonic school taught a refined doctrine of the higher cosmos or 'intelligible world' of entities transcending our five senses. At the summit of things stands the transcendent One; then, midway, the divine Mind; and thirdly the divine world-soul, immanent life force, explaining both the world's creative vitality and its controlled order. This divine Triad is graded in power and glory. Between the Triad and our earthly realm stands a whole hierarchy of intermediate beings, daemons or angels; the human body is created by intermediate beings, lower forms of animal life by inferior powers. Plato believed in reincarnation, a treadmill from which one should seek to find the way of liberation. Those who live evil lives may be condemned to return later, Plato and some Platonists (not Porphyry) thought to an animal or even in extreme cases vegetable life. Plotinus did not have room for divine grace in his thinking. There is no descent of the world-soul or Mind actively coming down to rescue man's soul from misery. But there is an undiminished giving, as sunlight is generated by the sun without loss to itself. And in the mutual relation of love, Plotinus discerned a reflection of the 'differentiation-and-identity' which is to be affirmed of the divine Triad. In God, he says (VI 8. 15. 1) love, the beloved, and the loving which returns upon its own origin, are one.

Not everything in the Platonic scheme struck an answering chord of sympathy in Early Christian hearts. Christians feared the notion that the soul is in the body now as a penalty for a wrong choice; since they believed the bonding of body and soul together in man to be the intention of the good Creator. They rejected the treadmill of reincarnation and the scarcely consistent belief that the soul in its true being belongs to the divine realm to which it should return. The very notion of world-cycles was uncongenially fatalist, and to the Christians not merely the body but the soul is created 'out of nothing', dependent for its existence on the will of God. The Christians welcomed the Platonic doctrine that the supreme God lies at the apex of all that is, but expressed his transcendence even more sharply. Augustine put it later in the formula that by 'God' we mean the highest good whence are derived all particular good things; without him nothing good would exist; and yet he is good without needing anything else to complete his being. The world contributes nothing to the transcendent being of its Maker.

Augustine heard these ideas being discussed in Simplician's circle at Milan. They offered a strong alternative to Manichee dualism and implied a wholly non-physical doctrine of the divine.

At the same time as his study of Plato, Augustine wrestled with the letters of St Paul, on which the Manichees much relied to support their dualism. He discovered the apostle could be better interpreted within a Platonic than a gnostic framework. But his reading of St Paul and experiments in using Plato as a key to unlock his obscurities did not yet mean an explicit or public association with the Church. Could he not purify his own soul and by Neoplatonic exercises lift his soul to eternal truth and union with God? His relationship to the Church was sufficiently protected by his resumption of the status of catechumen. His attempt at Neoplatonic mystical ecstasy, however, disappointed him by its transience.

## An Uncomfortable Call

One day Alypius and Augustine were called on by a brother African, a devout layman named Ponticianus, highly placed at the palace and therefore an influential person for the ambitious Africans to know. Picking up a book lying on Augustine's table Ponticianus was astonished to find a codex of St Paul's letters, not a book one expected in the hands of a municipal professor of rhetoric. He was moved to tell his friends about the monastic movement quietly growing in the western churches, including one house with brothers living a common life outside the walls of Milan itself under Ambrose's care. He told them how when the court was at Trier, two friends of his who were members of the secret police discovered a similar house with a Latin translation of Athanasius' *Life of St Anthony*. The reading of this work so inspired them that they renounced their career in the imperial service, where rewards were high but tenure precarious, and dedicated their lives to the ascetic way. (It was in just this kind of way that Jerome and his friend Bonosus were converted at Trier in the 370s, and they could conceivably be the two persons Ponticianus was referring to.)

Ponticianus' story left Augustine's mind in turmoil. He had thought such heroism occurred only in people of long ago. After Ponticianus had taken his leave, Augustine burst out in emotion: 'Simple folk are taking heaven by storm while we clever people without a heart wallow in the materialist world of flesh and blood.' Augustine describes how the lady Continence appeared to him, as if in a dream, and addressed him, with a surrounding company of boys and girls, calling him to be of her party. And now the moment of crisis came on fast. 'To reach my goal, I needed no chariot or ship' (a reminiscence of Plotinus) 'but a mere act of will.' Several times later in life Augustine will write of the suddenness of the will's turning at the hinge-point of conversion. Himself now at this hinge, he could not suppress a paroxysm of tears, and to spare embarrassment moved away from Alypius. Could he any longer echo the crow's cry 'Cras et cras', tomorrow and tomorrow (a reminiscence of Persius's fifth *Satire*). As he wept under a fig-tree (symbolic perhaps of Adam in the garden?), he heard a singing voice. Here the manuscripts of the *Confessions* vary between saying the voice came from the 'next-door house', which would seem a prosy thing to say unless it is simply factual reporting, and saying that it came from a 'house of God' (*vicina* against *divina*). The latter is the reading of much the oldest manuscript. If it is correct, there is probably a literary allusion to Psalm 42 (in Augustine's Latin Psalter, 41) 'As the hart longs for springs of water, so my soul longs for God . . .', where through his daily tears the distressed Psalmist 'poured out his soul' amid the voice of chanting at the house of God. A sermon on this Psalm which Augustine preached some years later has striking reminders of this passage of the *Confessions*.

The singing voice, 'whether of a boy or a girl I do not know', sings a refrain repeated over and over again, 'Take, read; take, read': *Tolle lege, tolle lege*. Augustine wondered, he says, if it could be an unfamiliar formula in a children's game. Or perhaps the innocent child was a member of the lady Continence's visionary choir, and the song echoed that sung by the ascetics of Revelation 14 who renounce marriage to follow the Lamb wherever he goes?

Augustine looked up and saw by Alypius the codex of St Paul's letters. Remembering an incident from the Life of St Anthony recounted by Ponticianus, when the saint is converted by the apparently fortuitous hearing of a Biblical text, he opened the book at random and lighted on Romans 13: 'Not in revellings and drunkenness, not in sexual indulgence and indecencies, not in contention and rivalry; but put on the Lord Jesus Christ and make no provision for the flesh in lusts.' The mature Augustine later expresses disapproval of sortilege or divination by random texts of the Bible (better perhaps the Bible than Virgil), though on one occasion when the Hippo reader read the wrong Psalm, Augustine took it to be a providential error and preached extempore on the text read. In 386 Augustine found a way out of his psychological deadlock by introducing a random element; the chance text acted as a liberator from an intolerable situation.

And now 'I had no wish to read more, nor was there need. At once a light of serenity flooded into my heart and all the darkness of doubt was dispelled.' At last he felt convinced that it was possible to realize the ascetic life. Alypius took the same decision of dedication, and the two passed indoors to tell the overjoyed

Monnica. It was much more than she had prayed for: her son not only desired to be an orthodox and baptized Christian, but no longer wished to pursue marriage and a secular career.

Augustine's exquisite telling of the garden scene has rich echoes and literary allusions. The reader aware of these harmonics in his ear is entitled to ask whether he is reading a purely factual narrative or a partly symbolist fiction. Of the fact of a turning-point in Augustine's personal quest there is no question; but its form is not plain prose but a subtle blending of symbolic overtones, some Platonic, some Biblical, some allusions to classical Latin literature.

Augustine a few weeks later confessed himself to feel like a man on a sea voyage who has, by providence, been driven to his desired haven by a storm when he was hardly heading in that direction as long as his own hand was at the helm. God had taken him by surprise. Tempest-tossed, he had seen in Ambrose his North Star; he has returned to himself and come home, *sua dulcissima patria* (*BV* 1. 2). 'Late have I loved you, O Beauty, ever new and yet how ancient' (*C* 10. 27. 38).

The *Confessions* are not the sole source for the story of Augustine's conversion, though they alone give the detailed narrative of the garden scene. The philosophical dialogues which he wrote during the next few months make several references to the change of direction that has come to his life. During the past century the learned have strenuously debated the historical evaluation of the *Confessions*, written thirteen or fourteen years later, in relation to the philosophical dialogues written within a few weeks of his conversion. There is a marked difference of tone, to which Augustine himself draws emphatic attention at one point in the *Confessions* (9. 4. 7). Already a bishop for two or three years when he wrote them, he disliked the urbane and worldly style of the early philosophical dialogues, even though they are expressly Christian in conviction. There is no solution in treating the dialogues as factual reporting and the *Confessions* as poetry since there is an equally strong literary, Ciceronian element in the dialogues. Augustine is a man who describes important events in his life by using a high style; that is his way of saying they are important.

The date of his conversion is about three weeks before the holiday period, fixed by law to start on 23 August. A harder matter to determine is the significance which he himself attaches to the event described. He does not represent it as a decisive move out of philosophical scepticism into an obedient acceptance of everything and anything the authority of the Church may now propose for his belief. He is open to listen with serious care to Ambrose's Lenten instruction, but is not yet at the stage of having grasped all that the Christian faith involves. Something of his own experience may be reflected in a letter he writes in 409 (*E* 102. 38) commenting on some objections to Christian belief taken from Porphyry: 'if an inquirer thinks he ought to settle absolutely every question, great or small, before becoming a Christian, he little appreciates the limitations of human life or of himself.' (Augustine agrees that there are a few large questions on which a decision is needed.) Pagan cult has had no foothold in his upbringing and background, so that he hardly needs to put that behind him, and his trust in astrology had already dropped away before he left Africa. He has no magical books to burn. He sees his conversion as the culmination of a moral and intellectual struggle, not as a flight from scepticism into the arms of authority. He has not yet acquired an articulate faith, but has turned his will so as to lead in that direction. Ambrose has convinced him of the incorporeality of God, and preached so profound a fusion of Christianity with Platonic mysticism that Augustine thinks of Christ and Plato as different teachers converging in the same truths, complementary to each other.

On the moral side, renunciation lies at the heart of his story; but it is not so much renunciation of sin as renunciation of the secular and so of marriage and sex. Every stream has come together in a great confluence to bring this about: Cicero's *Hortensius*, Neoplatonist ideals of the soul's ascent in emancipation from bodily distractions, readings in St Paul, brotherly pressure from Alypius, perhaps whatever it was inside him that for a decade made this highly intelligent man think it possible to be a Manichee—all these forces combined together to make his conversion to Christian orthodoxy a decision to live as a monk.

Only, for Augustine this cannot mean becoming a hermit like St Anthony in the Egyptian desert (*C* 10. 43. 70), or even knocking at the door of the recently founded house in the suburbs of Milan. Augustine's ascetic way is not to be that of Alypius whose dedication would lead him to such strenuous austerity that he walked barefoot even through the Italian winter, a form of mortification which in the late fourth-century churches of northern Italy and Spain is attested as giving rise to some controversy. Especially in Spain, critics of the practice regarded it as Manichee. Augustine wants to be a monk, but it must be in a community of brothers. For him solitude is a necessary periodic withdrawal, but not a normal road to truth, which is not something religious men find on their own. Because 'God's truth does not belong to any one man' (*C* 12. 25. 34), truth is found by a dialectic of question and answer. In any event at the natural level, Augustine is a born teacher who needs his pupils to get his own thinking clear.

One substantial element in Augustine's conversion is only marginally religious, namely a decision to make a shift from rhetoric to philosophy. For eight centuries past, ancient educational theorists had debated the relative value and priority of rhetoric as against philosophy. In the Latin West the debate had been less striking than in the Greek world, because rhetoric mattered much more in the lawcourts and in the political life of the State before it became a complete autocracy. The only philosophical education available in the West was that offered in schools of oratory. Augustine will now move across to the non-rhetorical camp (an anticipation of Boethius in AD 500). Philosophy in the Platonic tradition has become a consuming passion. The religious and philosophical quests are fused together in his mind, and this will remain true to the end of his life. Augustine brings philosophy and theology together in a way no earlier western Christian succeeded in doing. A century later Boethius will think the Augustinian synthesis too tight and wish to separate them a little to leave philosophy more autonomous.

# 2

# CASSICIACUM AND THE DEATH OF MONNICA AT OSTIA

Aᶠᵀᵉᴿ the emotional exhaustion of Augustine's inward struggles, the strain took its toll. He dragged himself through the remaining weeks of teaching duty. But his chest was giving him pain, breathing was difficult, his voice sank to a low whisper, and his eyes became inflamed. On top of that he had unpleasant toothache. More important, his teaching was increasingly felt to be unsatisfying. Was not much rhetoric the glossy purveying of lies? An orator is paid to plead a cause, not to uphold the truth. Augustine made an important concession to morality about which he had some qualms. He instructed his pupils that while they were morally entitled to use oratorical skill to gain acquittal for a defendant who was really guilty, they should never seek to secure the conviction of an innocent person. (Augustine's statement of this principle has had far-reaching influence in legal practice.) The main problem for him in the late summer of 386 was that he had ceased to respect his own calling. His panegyric on the emperor had been generously applauded by an audience of highly placed persons, all of whom knew as well as he did that the speech was a pack of lies and oily flattery. That was what was expected of a panegyrist before the emperor, and could any orator hope for a higher honour than to be invited to give such a speech? Augustine felt himself to be a salesman of sophistry. Secular ambition is about power and honour. Yet nothing can be more relative and precarious, the anxieties steadily increasing as one ascends the greasy pole until all the happiness one is seeking is at an end. So Augustine decided to resign his post at Milan. For the simpler life he would now lead, Romanianus' support would suffice.

As soon as the vacation began, Augustine together with Monnica, Adeodatus, Alypius, Nebridius, and a few other friends among the African colony were lent a villa belonging to a Milanese colleague of Nebridius, whose wife (not he) was a Christian. The villa lay in the foothills of the Alps at Cassiciacum (Cassago di Brienza, a little south of Como, 20 miles north of Milan). There they stayed about five months until it was time for Augustine to go to Milan to enter his name among the candidates for the Easter baptism over which Ambrose would preside on the night of 24–5 April 387. At Cassiciacum Augustine sought a withdrawal resembling that of Tusculum, the villa in the Alban hills where Cicero composed philosophical dialogues.

Augustine says (one cannot, of course, be sure that it is not literary fiction) that the discussions of the house-party at Cassiciacum were taken down by stenographers. Their tone is that of an urbane literary reading-party of gentle, humane scholars enjoying a pleasant light-heartedness and banter, cultivated conversation spiced with quotations from Virgil and allusions to Cicero, but underlying the whole a seriousness of purpose in the discovery of truth. It would be idle to pretend that the intellectual equipment of the miscellaneous company at Cassiciacum is the sharpest steel. The interest lies in what Augustine's leadership can make of them. Augustine is the professor, the others his pupils—except for his uneducated but wise mother, whose contributions to the dialogue are shrewd and practical. Monnica combines responsibility for their domestic comfort with the pastoral care of a spiritual director. Augustine assures her that women may become philosophers equal to men, and that all of them wish to learn from her wisdom.

The shorthand record became the basis of three short essays— on happiness, on the sceptical theory of knowledge (*Against the Academics*), and on the order of providence. They show how Augustine has gone back to the point where Cicero's *Hortensius* left him at the age of 19. To find happiness one must forgo the illusion that it is found in doing as one likes, since that means in practice the loss of any serious directing of oneself towards a moral ideal worthy of respect. But Augustine must also settle accounts with Cicero's sceptical thesis that, while probability is a sufficient guide for practical moral action, no principle or truth can be known with impregnable certainty. Augustine replies that words like 'false' or 'doubtful' or 'probable' or 'verisimilitude' have meaning only by implicit contrast with 'true'. To say of one's judgement that it must be sufficiently close to the truth to be a basis of action implies that somewhere there is truth for it to be like or unlike. We are rightly confident of mathematical propositions, and their certainty does not hang on the hesitancy attaching to sense-experience. Moreover 'I think, therefore I am'— or 'Even if I am mistaken, nevertheless I am.' In Augustine this famous formula, which he repeats many times in various writings, does not mean 'I am sure that I must exist or I could not doubt it.'

It is rather an assertion that in self-consciousness, in all human thought, there is a knowing which is purely mental apart from the empirical evidence of the five senses. That is to say, it is an intuition of the 'intelligible world', and therefore a foundation on which a Platonist may argue to the immateriality of the soul and the existence of God.

In the essays *On the Happy Life* and *Against the Academics* Cicero is at the centre of the stage, with Plato and Christ at the side. But Platonism is the dominant characteristic of the third Cassiciacum dialogue, *On Order*, an essay partly on providence and the problem of evil, partly on the liberal arts (grammar, rhetoric, logic, and the mathematical disciplines) as a ladder leading up to reflection on the soul and its origin in God. Augustine is still in process of shuffling off the rags of Manichaeism. Two approaches are adopted. On the one hand, evil is non-being. On the other hand, it is absorbed within a greater whole. We need to see it within an overmastering cosmic order, whose discordant elements may contribute to the grasp of a greater containing harmony. At the circumference of a sphere the whole cannot be grasped as it can from the centre (this image is in Plotinus). There is no conflict between Platonic philosophy and the authority of the Christian mystery, teaching that there is but one God who is Father, Son, and Holy Spirit, and that this God is so great as to take a human body, an act of divine humility very different from the pride of some intellectuals.

To these three dialogues Augustine appends his personal *Soliloquies*, in which the dialogue form is kept, the exchanges, however, being between Augustine and personified Reason. He invents the Latin word 'soliloquia' to describe his book, the most important of his works hitherto. The intention is to carry through in detail the argument that the way to the knowledge of God must be not by the investigation of his works in nature (though the design apparent even in fleas he thinks impressive), but by the cross-examination through introspection of the human soul. The *Soliloquies* begin with a very long prayer to God which in content is an inextricable fusion of Platonic and Christian. Its form directly anticipates that of the later *Confessions*. The theme is announced in the declaration 'I desire to know God and the soul. Nothing more? Absolutely nothing.' By a careful dialectical method Augustine examines the nature of knowledge. The soul has its own eye (so Plato had said), and God is the sun giving it light to see by. In Augustine, as already in Plotinus, the old Platonic doctrine of the soul dimly remembering divine truths from its pre-bodily past is quietly replaced by a doctrine of divine illumination. But the Augustine of the *Soliloquies* is sure that the soul needs not only the purging of earthly desires but also the presence of faith, hope, and charity, which is the enjoyment of its object 'with no veil between', that is the vision of God.

Reason questions Augustine about his future. It is good that he eats frugally. It may well be a justified decision to remain unmarried, a matter on which Reason is open to conviction. Augustine confesses that he has not yet gained control of his imagination, and expresses dread that the dark forces within him may still captivate him by pleasure. In the *Confessions* more than ten years later he prays God that his dream-life may be made more chaste, and confesses himself still uncertain what hidden impulses lie within. (*C* 10. 30. 41). There may be an autobiographical touch, however, in a sentence of 401 (*BC* 21. 25) 'Many find complete abstinence easier than moderation.' However, in 386 he can only aspire towards Reason's expectations of him. Money has never been important to him, and the resignation of his professorship is clearly a step in the right direction. But Reason is surprised at the plan to establish a monastic community of friends and pupils. Must not the presence of others hinder private mysticism? Augustine concedes they may prove a distraction (*Solil.* 1. 12. 20). Indeed he has written these private soliloquies addressed to himself to avoid those feelings of pride and resentment which enter into arguments between people, each being reluctant to admit himself mistaken (*Solil.* 2. 7. 14). But the discovery of truth is a corporate enterprise in which we need each other's criticism and help. Divine truth is true in a sense transcending that of particular statements about specific objects in space and time. That the soul is immortal is a proposition which Reason demonstrates to Augustine by the argument of Plato (*Meno* 86 B) that the soul has the capacity to know things that are eternally true.

The *Soliloquies* represent the most advanced and weighty piece among the Cassiciacum dialogues. His friends there did not understand the book, and to help them Augustine composed a private tract on the immortality of the soul. Like other such elucidations, it is more obscure than the text it seeks to explain, and Augustine himself looked back on the tract without pleasure. He evidently felt that he needed to discipline the minds of his friends by more preliminary training. The essay *On Order* gives a highly positive role to the liberal arts in training the mind to grasp dialectical arguments and, through mathematical studies, to comprehend immaterial realities. Augustine began a series of handbooks to each of the liberal arts in turn—grammar, rhetoric, dialectic, and music (this last being more about metre than sound). Arguments drawn from geometry appear in several essays of this period (especially the first book of the *Soliloquies* and a book on whether the soul has size, *De quantitate animae*); and although the work on geometry is quite lost he probably wrote something on the subject. In 427 he could not find the manuscript of his *Grammar*. It had been 'borrowed' from his library, sure evidence that one of the brothers thought it a useful work.

During his preparation for baptism Augustine was recommended by Ambrose to read the prophet Isaiah. He found the book beyond his comprehension, but was undiscouraged. Together with Adeodatus and Alypius he was baptized at Easter 387. About this time the little African colony at Milan was joined by another friend from Thagaste named Euodius. Converted and baptized at some earlier time, he now gave up a good post in the administration to join Augustine's ascetic circle. A decision was made that the brothers should return to Africa and set up their house there. Augustine and Monnica moved south to Rome and then, while waiting for their ship, to the quiet town of Ostia on the coast away from the hubbub of both Rome and its nearby port. Unfortunately in the summer of 387 civil war broke out; the sea was closed to traffic.

At Ostia Monnica fell sick, and after nine days of fever died. She was 56. Shortly before the fever seized her, she had had a presentiment of the proximity of death and told Augustine that, since his baptism, her work was done; she did not need to live further, and could happily say her *Nunc dimittis*. At a high climax of the *Confessions* (9. 10. 23–5) Augustine describes, in a passage of exquisite prose with reminiscences of Plotinus how, two or three days before the fever attacked her, Monnica and he were speaking together of the soul's ascent beyond all earthly things, to the realms beyond space and time where there is no successiveness of past and future but an eternal Now. The timeless Word of God contrasts with our transient time-conditioned speech. If we set aside all that is passing away in man and his environment, the material universe, the visions and dreams of man's image-making mind, all the turmoil of words, so as to contemplate in silence, in reason's ear we hear the created order telling us that man does not make himself. If, then, in this silence of all earthly things, we listen for the very voice of God immanent in his creation, no created thing intervening, 'at that moment we reach our very selves and in a flash of thought touch the eternal abiding Wisdom beyond all things'.

Augustine adds that he has not here reproduced exactly the words used at the time. That the dialectical ascent which this passage describes remains important to him can be seen from its reproduction in a letter of 410 (*E* 120. 2. 11–12).

Monnica had wished to be buried beside her husband. At Ostia she realized it would not be so. But 'nothing is far from God; there is no fear that he will not know where I am at the resurrection of the dead'. A verse epitaph was later composed for her tomb by an admirer of the *Confessions*, the consular Anicius Bassus. Until 1945 this epitaph was known only through a copy made by a medieval pilgrim. In 1945 two boys playing basketball dug a hole in the ground for their post, and unearthed a piece of marble with part of the original inscription.

In the closing pages of the ninth book of the *Confessions* Augustine writes of her funeral, of the eucharist in celebration of the sacrifice of our redemption offered on her behalf, and of his own prayer for her peace. With her burial the autobiographical narrative of the *Confessions* ends. An element in the motivation leading to the writing of the book is clearly his acknowledgement of debt to her. He had found her possessive at one stage of his life and had been forced to take his liberty against her wishes. But he was deeply moved when on her deathbed she told him she could remember no harsh word against her on his lips. In Augustine's mind she almost takes on the qualities and epithets of Mother Church.

# 3

# BACK TO THAGASTE

THE continuing civil war made it impossible to return to Africa before the sailing season closed. With Euodius and other African friends Augustine lived quietly in Rome. The stay gave him the opportunity to meet some of the aristocratic Christian families concerned for the ascetic life, but he was not now holding any position of public consequence and there was no special reason why anyone should pay special attention to him. The Roman stay gave him opportunity to study divergent customs between Africa, Rome, and Milan. At Milan Monnica had tried to continue her African ways and offered food and wine at martyrs' shrines; she was rebuked by Ambrose who had put a stop to all wine-drinking at feast-days. Yet at St Peter's Rome Augustine found drinking wine a daily occurrence by the shrines of Peter and Paul (*E* 29. 10), and was shocked. It was explicable (he felt) only because St Peter's is so far from the Pope's residence on the Lateran or because the place is beset by vast crowds of tourists bringing their customs from elsewhere; surely it cannot be a native Roman practice. In his later attempts to clean up African celebrations of martyrs, the Roman practice was tellingly cited against his reforming zeal.

Roman custom was to fast on Saturday (apparently in com-memoration of an incident in the conflict between St Peter and Simon Magus described in the apocryphal *Acts of Peter* as occurring on a Saturday). A handful of African churches also did so, but only a tiny minority, and no Eastern church kept such a fast. Milan did not. At Monnica's request in 385 Augustine had gone to Ambrose to ask the reason for the divergence. Ambrose regarded the issue as a matter of indifference, and his advice was 'when in Rome do as Rome does'; but not at Milan. The Manichee provincial in Augustine was a little baffled at the time by so sophisticated an answer which offered him no reason in the ordinary sense. Later he appreciated its wisdom. When he became bishop he never thought uniformity in liturgical usage to be in the least necessary. He regretted it when clergy bewildered their congregations by introducing liturgical customs which they had seen when abroad. Admittedly he did not wholly keep his own advice, and soon found that a bishop has no more bitter critic than a conservative layman offended by liturgical change (*R* 2. 11).

To return to Rome was to come back to the city where he had been closely associated with the Manichees. In 387–8 he wrote there further works of anti-Manichee polemic on the problem of evil and the nature of the soul, and especially began a substantial work *On Freedom of Choice* (*De libero arbitrio*). This work he discovered later to be widely read. To the end of his life he defended its argument as his best statement on providence, evil, and freedom, and disclaimed the appeals made to it by his Pelagian critics. He was particularly interested in the little communities of ascetics in the city which had received vigorous impetus, and some embarrassing patronage, from Jerome a few years previously (382–5). Jerome, a prickly character with a brilliant pen and acid in his ink, eventually provoked a storm of protest against his activities, and left for the East pursued by horrid charges of Manichaeism and questionable relationships with some of the aristocratic ladies who looked to him for spiritual direction. But Augustine found congenial matter for his own purposes in Jerome's 22nd letter on virginity which had much upset many in the capital. Augustine reports that Rome possessed substantial ascetic societies of men and of women, in each case led by a wise director, supporting themselves by manual labour. Although from Jerome's 22nd letter he knows about Egypt's hermits, the common life of small groups attracts his interest. This is the right kind of organization for realizing the Platonic and Stoic ideal of the wise man, educated in liberal arts and philosophy and now to be formed in personal life by the example of Christ.

This is the ideal with which Augustine returns to Africa. Hitherto the African churches possessed ascetics continuing to live with their families and perhaps the occasional half-hermit, but no monasteries living a common life. The return to Africa in August or September 388 marked the end of Augustine's overseas travels. He was never again to leave African soil. The return brought some regrouping among the circle of friends. Nebridius, who had been slower than Augustine in coming forward for baptism, fell sick and went back to his family home near Carthage where he soon died, filling Augustine with grief. Augustine, Alypius, and Euodius settled with a handful of others at Thagaste. A few months later Augustine sold his share of the modest family estate and gave the money to the local church for the poor. All the brothers at Thagaste were laymen, and totalled about ten or a dozen. The atmosphere was like that of Cassiciacum, exploring the coming together of Plato and Christianity under the intellectual guidance of Augustine's restless mind. Thagaste offered withdrawal from the tumult to a philosophical contemplation, 'the (outward and inward) tranquillity to enable the soul to become divine' (*deificari in otio*, *E* 10. 2), with regular hours of prayer and silence and shared psalmody. Augustine never speaks of the house as a monastery nor of monks; they are 'brothers'. But in fact he was fast creating a monastery, and six years later express evidence appears of *monasteria* under this title at Carthage, Hippo, and Thagaste.

The Thagaste brothers formed the custom of putting questions to Augustine. Eighty-three of these questions with his answers came to be preserved on loose sheets; forty years later Augustine gave them numbers for ease of reference and 'published' the collection (i.e. allowed copies to be made for circulation). They are virtually in chronological order, so that the reader can trace the shifting of Augustine's mind from a predominant concern with Neoplatonic logic and philosophical theology to his first struggles with the higher mountains of New Testament interpretation. His early fragments of exposition of St Paul and St John suggest access to Greek interpretations (Irenaeus, Origen, Gregory of Nazianzus, Gregory of Nyssa) as well as to the familiar Latin texts of Tertullian and Hilary of Poitiers. The house evidently possessed a small but good library. If one of the brothers was Greek-speaking, he may have given Augustine oral help with the Greek texts. Conflict with Manichaeism appears in several of the answers. There are also echoes of anti-Arian argument which must echo the Milanese experience of Ambrose's conflicts with the emperor's Arian mother Justina, since Arians in Africa are rare until the fifth century.

## Language and Communication

Within a year of the settlement at Thagaste in 388 Augustine's son Adeodatus died. There is no record to tell whether his mother came from Carthage for the requiem customary on the seventh day after death. On the basis of the boy's discussions with his father and as his memorial, Augustine wrote a book, *The Teacher* (*De magistro*), which centuries later became profoundly influential in medieval schools. The essay concerns the ways in which we communicate with one another. Its thesis is highly paradoxical.

Our chief method of communication is (we suppose) by words. Words can be used for other purposes; e.g. we like singing to ourselves without wanting to tell anyone anything thereby. Spoken words are signs, written words signs of signs. But how do they transmit information? The process is more complex than people imagine. Meaning is conveyed not so much by individual words as by sentences, by paragraphs, by longer units of discourse; the meaning of a word depends on the entire sentence, that of the sentence on the entire paragraph, etc., and even then some of the underlying structure of presuppositions may not be articulated at all. But information may also be conveyed without words: by gestures, by miming, by the rise and fall of our voice as we speak, by facial expression. Augustine notes elsewhere that sometimes we adopt a facial expression which tells our hearers we are being ironic. He was also intrigued by the use of idiomatic phrases to mean the exact opposite of what they profess to say, e.g. in African idiom 'abundat', 'there is any amount of it', was what men said to indicate they had not got any at all. and the goods were out of stock. So communication is no simple matter of knowing how to construe a sentence.

How do we know what a man means? Not so much by what he says as by what he does. Actions, moreover, can be at least as communicative as words. This bears on our tests for the sincerity of what we are being told. If an Epicurean philosopher expounds to us the immortality of the soul, we may deduce from his Epicureanism that he himself does not believe it, whatever he may say on the subject. (Augustine remarks in the *Confessions* how attractive he would have found Epicurus' philosophy if only he had not denied the immortality of the soul.) Liars use words to convey information intended to mislead. Therefore there is a wide gap between thought and language. Moreover, thought moves faster than it can be articulated in speech. In a slip of the tongue we say one thing with our mouth while the mind imagines we have said something different. When singing a familiar hymn, our minds may wander away from the words on our lips. So words, for all their importance and utility, are not the only or even principal thing. From the proposition that we learn by conventional signs, Augustine moves to the surprising thesis that by mere signs we learn nothing important at all. Logic, moreover, teaches us how inaccurate much of our everyday way of speaking can be; an area where usage is decisive (as Augustine adds, echoing Horace). We communicate truth not by verbal or non-verbal signs but by an interior experience of a sharing of minds.

In prayer we use words but well know that they do not inform God of anything he does not know or can conceivably have forgotten. 'True prayer is in the silent depths of the soul.' In the Lord's Prayer Christ taught us not a mere formula but realities of which the words are signs. At the everyday level there can be problems in conveying one's true thought to another person's mind. For a variety of reasons one may be heard as saying something other than what one intends. But in any event no one can grasp meaning just from words as merely external sounds or symbols. They are a medium between rational minds, a system of reminders. Our minds are by creation rational. There is implanted in humanity the capacity for reason which is the image of God in man. Education is drawing out what the pupil's mind already possesses within him, and a teacher has a far more subordinate role than he and others suppose. He is a medium through which his pupils are introduced not to his personal thoughts, but to the branch of knowledge being studied, and once they have grasped it they do not need him. Augustine's formulation here evidently reflects the tiny debt which he felt himself to owe to his own teachers rather than to the books to which they may have introduced him. Effective instruction is not achieved by one person talking and everyone else listening (*EP* 139. 15).

The very possibility of learning, then, depends on the interior reason, and that is ultimately a divine illumination. Education, when you inquire into its first principles, presupposes theology, a God-given capacity for communion of minds beyond the merely external use of sounds and symbolic acts.

Augustine also feels the inadequacy of word to thought, and of thought to something lying deeper than the upper levels of the mind we call intellect. Twenty years later he returns in a sermon to the relation between words, thoughts, and feelings: 'Man can say nothing of what he is unable to feel, but he can feel what he is unable to say' (*S* 117. 5. 7–8). Something of the same idea is reflected both in the *Confessions* and in his work *On the Trinity*, where he speaks of the phenomenon of what we would call the subconscious: 'you know something you do not know that you know.' The same attitude appears in his repeated descriptions of philosophical truth acquired by ingenious dialectic as 'doctrine without heart' (C 8. 8. 19 and elsewhere).

For the words of the Bible, however, Augustine had great respect. He expressly denies that inspiration means they can be other than human and expressed in language accommodated to human capacity. But within these human words man hears the word of God. The text of Scripture is capable of many diverse interpretations, any of which is acceptable provided that it is not heretical. The gift of grace is to discern the inwardness of God's word.

So also the sacraments of baptism and eucharist are 'visible words' (F 19. 16), never to be despised because they are external acts; yet the words they make visible are addressed to faith. 'Without faith baptism does not profit.' There must also be an inward conversion through which is given citizenship of the heavenly city. The eucharistic memorial of Christ's passion is likewise, to faith, the offering in which Christ is himself both priest and victim and also the offering of the Church by the Church in self-offering. It is also that through which Christ gives to his faithful his very self in the consecrated bread and wine. But sacraments are not magic. They must be received in faith. 'Believe and you have eaten' (crede et manducasti: TJ 25. 12). The bread and wine, set apart and designated in the eucharist, symbolize and make a reality of the believer's incorporation in the Church, so that 'we may be what we receive' (S 57. 7. 7). That is because Christ makes them his own, and so the eucharist is no sacrifice other than Christ's and no gift other than that of Christ himself (S 227; EP 48. 1. 3).

## *True Religion*

Among the most remarkable of Augustine's pieces written in the lay community at Thagaste in 390 is an essay entitled *On True Religion* (*De vera religione*), which he dedicated to his benefactor Romanianus. Twenty-five years later he would restate much of its argument in the *City of God*. What Plato saw dimly and taught to an elite few, Christ has made clear and universally accessible. Many Platonists are now becoming Christians. Platonic idealism and Christianity are often thought incompatible for the reason that Christian faith is more obviously rooted in discerning God in nature and history than in searching for the supreme Being beyond time and space. But Platonism too teaches that man is fallen by a freely chosen preference for the lower and material instead of the higher good. The turmoil of history, the mess of events so alien to some Platonists, fits into place when one sees that it is like an epic poem. Because we ourselves are actors in the story, we cannot see it as a whole. But through its purging, the righteous and the impious are shown up for what they are. Divine revelation is an education of humanity to ascend through and from the temporal to the eternal. We should not set aside the created order as evil since everything, even the lowest of beings, has its place and its own beauty—apart, of course, from evils resulting from man's free choices. And even human vices are perversions of something good, and are essentially parasitic upon virtue.

# 4
# DISCOVERING THE CHURCH

AUGUSTINE did not travel about much during his time as a layman at Thagaste; if he did go about visiting, he was careful to avoid any town where they needed a new bishop since pressure might suddenly be put upon him. Early in 391, however, he visited the harbour-town of Hippo Regius, forty miles away, a town with fine buildings and enjoying prosperity, though always second fiddle to Carthage among African cities. Carthage was the acknowledged metropolis, the 'caput Africae' (*E* 43. 6. 17), the best centre of literary and humane culture that Africa could show. (*E* 118. 2. 9 shows Augustine in 410 rather enjoying the absurdity of a bright young man disappointed with the level of culture he has found at Carthage or even Rome, turning to an overworked bishop at an unpretentious provincial town to find the real thing.) Augustine went to Hippo in answer to an invitation from a layman who said he wished to consult him on a religious problem. The little Catholic community at Hippo had a bishop in good health, Valerius, who was a Greek-speaker with hesitant Latin originally from South Italy whither he needed to go from time to time to look after his family land. Augustine courteously called on Valerius to pay his respects.

Valerius' Sunday sermon expressly welcomed the visitor from Thagaste and then reminded the congregation how much he needed a presbyter to assist and to deputize for him. Augustine found all eyes on him. Amid rising uproar the people allowed him no escape and, despite his profound reluctance, forthwith compelled him to accept ordination at Valerius' hands. Those who saw his tears supposed him disappointed in his ambitions for a bishopric.

To a layman who had renounced the turmoil of the world to adopt the contemplative life in a Platonic–Christian community, and whose health remained precarious, the responsibility thrust upon him was highly unwelcome. Some weeks afterwards he was writing to Valerius that the Hippo ordination was a punishment for his sins, to which of course he submitted. Never did it occur to him or anyone else that he had a moral right to refuse a divine calling issued even in such a manner through the Church of God. 'None may dare to refuse the sacrament of ordination' (QH 4. 54; FO 17. 32). He must obey, but asked leave of Valerius to stay on at Thagaste until Easter to give himself time for Bible study and prayer (E 21. 3–4). Does one give the post of deputy pilot to a sailor who had not yet learnt to handle an oar? Augustine felt himself to be a danger both to the Church and to himself because of his ignorance and unfitness. Moreover, how could his monastic vocation be reconciled with countless administrative cares sure to distract him both from and in his prayers? Augustine was still in process of discovering that ordinary churches are not places where half-educated fools imagine they worship God while the wise men are in a country villa studying oriental mysticism and Plotinus. His first act at Hippo was a Lenten catechetical lecture on the creed delivered in mid-March 391. The text survives

(*S* 214) and shows how profitable his crash course in divinity had been to him.

## Still a Monk

Augustine was determined not to abandon his monastic dedication after moving to Hippo. Valerius offered Augustine a garden by the church as a building-site for a small monastery, to which the Thagaste community sent a few brothers including Euodius and, for a time, Alypius to start it off. But the Hippo community was not like the highbrow philosophical society which came to Thagaste in 388. The majority were slaves, freedmen, peasants, manual workers. Slaves were accepted only with their owner's consent and therefore (unless their master was outstandingly devout and in special circumstances) tended to be elderly and infirm. Not all came from Hippo (*E* 64. 3). The laity much outnumbered the clergy recruits, clergy again tending to come there in old age. Illiterates were taught letters, to take part in the daily readings and psalmody. The society was slow to have its procedures formalized. As late as 405 a letter from Augustine to Alypius (who became bishop of Thagaste in 394) shows him feeling his way, as a result of an embarrassing controversy, towards the fixed rule that the property of a monk at entry must be formally assigned to the community; and if he brought with him money properly belonging to his family, that portion should be returned to them forthwith. There is no record of explicit vows of either obedience or chastity, though both must have been self-evident conditions of membership. An entrant to the monastery was understood to be a trainee for service in Christ's army; but there was no novitiate, so that, if he then left, it would not be without a sense of being a failure (*E* 243). Augustine was much against the ordination of 'deserter' monks (*E* 60. 1), language which shows how he felt about the nature of the commitment.

His monks soon had a recognizable style of simple cap and cloak (*EP* 147. 8). By 401 there were complaints of the dress characteristic of monks being worn by wandering confidence tricksters and salesmen of bogus relics of martyrs (*OM* 28. 36). All the monks' work was done for the community. Domestic responsibilities were apportioned among them, some cooking, others caring for the sick, others copying books or no doubt acting as shorthand writers for the ceaselessly dictating Augustine. The more strenuous monks slept on hard pallets and in penitential discipline might practise self-flagellation (*J* 6. 15. 46). Hermits lie quite outside Augustine's purview, though by 397 he is well aware of their existence on rocky offshore islands in the western Mediterranean 'full of faith, hope, and charity' but with no copy of the Bible. In 397 he corresponded with the abbot of a house on Capraria by Sardinia. The Rule which Augustine wrote for his monks at Hippo is the earliest of all monastic rules in the West; it was known to St Benedict 130 years later.

Augustine recalled that the illiterate St Anthony had learnt the Bible by heart. Such feats were not unknown at this time. Augustine even tells of one well-educated African friend with so prodigious a memory that he could recite Virgil backwards (cite any line and he could at once recite the preceding one, and so back to the beginning) and could declaim whole orations of Cicero. Augustine expected not only hermits to memorize their Bible. Monks at Hippo were encouraged to learn substantial portions by heart. There is no doubt that Augustine did so himself.

In the 390s the monastery for men was paralleled by a house for women, in the charge of one given the title 'mother', with a presbyter to care for their pastoral and liturgical needs. The sisters too had an identifiable dress. Widows were accepted into this community, one being Augustine's sister. Augustine specially mentions the work in rescuing foundlings. In 401 he composed a treatise *On Holy Virginity* to inspire the sisters with the dignity of their high calling. By being born of Mary the Lord has sanctified both sexes equally. The nun free of family ties takes Mary as her model, and follows the Lamb wherever he goes. (Augustine's connected development of these two themes may, one suspects, lie behind a well-known nursery rhyme.) The theme of the nun as Christ's bride, embarrassing to modern feminists, was already part of the ascetic vocabulary of dedication when Augustine wrote. He treats it with more care and taste than Jerome had done. The nunnery tended to recruit women from a higher social class than the male monastery, and this caused difficulties. Poor recruits thereby acquired security and a comfort never previously known; the well-connected secretly resented giving all their wealth to the community. With surprise Augustine records that avarice is not easy to eradicate from either rich or poor even among ascetics.

## Is the Monastery Manichee?

The rise of the monastic movement in the fourth century did not occur without opposition. Bishops understandably distrusted a movement which took some of the most devout Christians away from ordinary congregations and segregated them in societies inclined to look down on normal church life as 'secular' and bedevilled by moral compromises. In some cases there was a well-grounded suspicion that these ascetics who thought sex evil and drank no wine were in heart and perhaps in mind Manichees. That the ascetic movement was infiltrated by gnostic theosophy is certain. At Pachomius' earliest of all monasteries sharing a common life, in the Nile valley, bizarre books like the texts found near Nag-Hammadi were read for edification. In 367 Athanasius of Alexandria issued a list of canonical books of the Bible with warnings that outside this list reading should be carefully restricted. The apocryphal Acts of Thomas or Paul or others were stamped with obviously Manichee doctrines and were widely diffused in both East and West. In Spain in the 370s and 380s fierce controversy was precipitated by an evangelical ascetic movement led by Priscillian, bishop of Ávila from 381, executed about 385 by the emperor Magnus Maximus on charges of sorcery and Manichaeism brought against him by a brother bishop from the Algarve. Jerome, as we have seen, left Rome quickly in 385 because similar charges were being levelled against him.

Augustine's decision to establish and diffuse monasticism in Africa took risks of provoking opposition. The rival community of Donatists (below, pp. 105–15) laughed at the to them strange notion, and mocked the unfamiliar word 'monachi', monks. Augustine's explanation of the Greek word to mean 'only one' glosses this to make it refer to the united dedication of the monks in common life, and says nothing about hermits living alone. The Donatists may well have thought that Augustine was trying to create a brigade of Catholic shock-troops to answer their own ascetic Circumcellions (pp. 101–4). Augustine's Hippo monastery was seized on by critics as evidence of the rags of Manichaeism still hanging about him.

Accordingly Augustine's writings during his five or six years' service as a presbyter at Hippo are mainly polemic against the Manichees. He wrote brief expositions of the beginning of Genesis, both allegorical and also literal, to show that it is not indispensable to allegorize these chapters to rescue them for edification—a theme which he took up later (401–14) in a big book, the *Literal Commentary on Genesis* in which anti-Manichee polemic yields to a highly Neoplatonic understanding of creation and the soul. He also wrote commentaries on Romans and Galatians, letters of Paul to which Manichees delighted to appeal. In a substantial essay called *The Utility of Believing* he tried to convert to orthodoxy a friend named Honoratus whom he had once carried with him into Manichaeism. The argument turns on the relation between authority and reason, whether in religion or in any other kind of assent. There is no argument in which the very first principles and primary axioms can actually be established by reason. Without trust human life is unworkable. Authority and reason are not antithetical or contradictory. If we demand rational demonstration before assenting to anything, chaos will ensue. To find religious truth, we need to associate ourselves with those who make good claim to have it, and in Christ believers see the wisdom of God, the summit of authority and reason in one. Both Church and Bible point to him. It is not unreasonable to start from there, just as sensible people do not dispute that Cicero is the best model for Latin oratory. The body that speaks to us of Christ is the Church; all sects agree that there can be only one Catholic Church, whose continuity with the apostolic community is visible through the ordered succession of bishops. Divine providence, evident in the order of the heavens and the moral law acknowledged by the conscience, would not have left humanity without sufficient guidance to find the way. Belief in Christ's authority is vindicated by the miraculous expansion of Christianity in the world, by the argument from the fulfilment of prophecy, and by the wonders done by Christ. To trust the authority of the community that bears this witness is anything but irrational. Augustine loves to quote Isa. 7: 9 in the old Latin version: 'Unless you believe, you will not understand.'

The essay for Honoratus is a sketch for a fuller development in a work written not longer after he had become a bishop, a *Refutation of Mani's Fundamental Epistle*, where the argument is made to ring out like a challenge: 'I would not have believed the gospel unless the authority of the Catholic Church had constrained me to do so'—where Augustine is appealing not to a centralized authority but to the universality of shared belief.

In arguing with Manichees Augustine does not appeal to anything they do not themselves acknowledge, and for the most part his controversial ground is an appeal to reason. It is in this context of anti-Manichee polemic that he makes his famous remark 'Hear the other side' (*Audi partem alteram*: DA 22).

### Ethics

About 393–4 he wrote an exposition of the Sermon on the Mount, parts of which touch on the Manichee controversy. The Manichees expounded Jesus' words about the good tree producing good fruit, the bad tree bad, to teach the ultimate dualism of good and evil natures—a doctrine which they also found in St Paul in Romans 7. Augustine tells his readers to be on their guard. His exposition gives occasion for a wider examination of Christian conduct, with much positive matter free from controversial preoccupations. Augustine wants his readers to have a better understanding of what the Lord intends them to think and do about prayer, or how they are to treat their obstreperous neighbour, or what is the Christian duty in regard to divorce and remarriage. He takes the Lord to mean that inward intention rather than outward act is that which gives moral value to what we do. In a recent instance a noble wife extricated her husband from prison and death by being willing to sleep with his powerful tormentor, an act of love and loyalty to her husband. Elsewhere Augustine remarks on the courage and loyalty which some wives have shown precisely when their husbands have fallen into the deepest trouble: 'Proscription has made some the more loved by their wives' (*EP* 55. 17).

Augustine's argument about the intention and the situation being decisive in estimating the rightness and wrongness of an act is one which he takes a long way. An untrue statement is a moral crime if intended to deceive, but not if no one is being deceived or if one makes a mistake in good faith. You should tell the truth; but you are not obliged to say all that is in your heart if it may do harm to say it. Oaths should be avoided, but are acceptable when you would not otherwise be believed. To swear truly is no sin; to support a lie by an oath adds to the offence. To undress at the baths is inoffensive, at a lascivious party it is wicked. Men who don female dress forfeit social respect, and by Roman law transvestism is forbidden. But to serve one's country in war by using it as a disguise or to keep warm in icy weather because no other than feminine clothing is available cannot be censured. Not all homicide is sin absolutely. A judge may have to pass the death sentence (though Augustine earnestly hopes he will find a way of avoiding it), and a soldier may fight in a just war (as the lesser of two evils) for the peace of the world at the command of the emperor to whom in any event obedience is owed. To say otherwise would be to leave men to take the law into their own hands, and nothing could be worse than that. 'The wars of a Christian state must be so conducted that after conquest the conquered enemy may enjoy peace, justice, and piety' (*E* 138. 2. 14).

Slavery as an institution is a tragic consequence of man's fallen estate which is the cause of one man's dominance over his fellow-men. The fact that the institution of slavery, evil as it is, helps to preserve order in human society suggests to Augustine that it is a penalty God has imposed for the fall of Adam which nevertheless has some beneficial side-effects. But it is wicked to treat slaves as chattels: they are not to be treated as disposable means—they are, as human beings, ends to be loved. 'A good master does not need his slave; the slave needs him' (*E* 138. 1. 6). Augustine records with some outrage that a slave costs much less than a racehorse (*CD* 11. 16). (In his time the average price of an unskilled slave would have been about three times that of a cart-horse for farm work.)

In a number of contexts Augustine formulates a general principle: provided your motive is wholly altruistic, you may say or do what you please. 'Love and do as you like' (*Dilige et quod vis fac*: *EJ* 7. 8), a saying he usually applies to the administering of rebuke or correction. 'Doves are loving even through a quarrel; a wolf, smooth with flattery, is filled with hate' (*S* 64. 7).

An essential duty prescribed in scripture for all Christians is almsgiving. To fail here 'resembles fraud' (*S* 206. 2). Yet no more difficult duty can be found. First, know that when you give alms, you do so because you share with the beggar a common humanity, and you give not to the beggar only but to Christ in him. Your Master did not just give money to the poor and hope they would soon go away. He identified himself with God's poor. Some rich people give alms proportionate to their sins, which is no bad principle as long as they remember that, if wealth was obtained by oppression, it will never win remission to offer even a tiny fragment of their resources to the poor. Augustine wisely observes that in charitable giving it is a good thing to take your wife into your confidence, and deplores the suggestion that when Jesus told his disciples not to let their left hand know what their right hand does, he meant them to keep their wives in the dark about such things.

Accordingly, the moral value of an action depends on the motive, on the situation, and on the end for which it is done. A failure properly to distinguish between ends and means will be found, he thinks, to be the most fertile of all sources of ethical confusion. An end is that which we should 'enjoy' for its own sake; the means we use are distinct. Human corruption sets in as soon as people try to make use of ends and treat mere means as if they may be properly enjoyed as ends.

The distinction beween enjoyment and use turns up in many places in Augustine's writings, and is especially developed in the work *On Christian Teaching* begun soon after he had become a bishop (below, pp. 82–6). Here he surprises his readers by working out a parallel between ends and means on the one hand and love to God and one's neighbour on the other, as if God the Holy Trinity is alone a proper end, while one's neighbour can be used as a means. Elsewhere Augustine makes another and happier parallel between ends and means on the one hand and the contrast between contemplative and active on the other (*CE* i,8), the practical being, for any Platonist, properly subordinate to the contemplative. A passage of Cicero distinguished between goods sought for their own sake, goods sought for the sake of their consequences, and goods sought for both reasons. The passage so fascinated Augustine that he included it as one of his answers to the eighty-three questions asked by the brothers at Thagaste (*DQ* 31). It mediates to him the discussion of the subject, which he had never read, in Plato's *Republic*. For Augustine the distinction merges into his view of the temporal as that which we must pass through to reach the things eternal. Everything short of the enjoyment of the final goal in God becomes a subordinate object of our love, and in that sense is 'used' (by which Augustine does not mean 'exploited').

# 5

# BISHOP

A T some date between 4 May 395 and 28 September 397, and probably in 396 (the evidence for a precise date is lacking), Augustine was consecrated coadjutor bishop of Hippo side by side with the now ageing Valerius. A neighbouring church whose bishop had died had sent to Hippo a snatch-party to try and persuade or kidnap Augustine to come as their bishop. Augustine successfully hid himself. But the incident alarmed Valerius, who wished for Augustine as his successor. In the fourth century several instances occurred of bishops, when nearing their end, nominating a successor rather than leaving the matter to the electoral process, which was often divisive and could tear the flock apart into rival factions that might even come to blows. The business of normal election gave a considerable voice to the local clergy and people, controlled only by their need to persuade the other bishops of the province, especially their presiding figure or metropolitan, to accept their selected candidate and to lay hands on his head with prayer. Human nature being what it is, disagreement was a normal condition in a diocese when a see fell vacant, and the results could be unedifying. Rival candidates tended to be backed by different party groups or powerful family interests. Payments to obtain ecclesiastical office were utterly forbidden as the sin of Simon Magus who thought he could buy the gift of the

Holy Spirit with money (a prohibition in strong contrast to the secular empire where no substantial position could be obtained without money quietly passing). But it was deemed permissible to bid for the support of the poor, for whom the church chest controlled by the bishop was a crucial source of welfare, by promises of special distributions. These would have to be financed by the sale of church plate or endowments of property given by wealthy but dead benefactors. In the ancient Church, as in modern secular democracies, one must on no account bribe the electors with one's own money, but it is acceptable to bribe them with their own.

Evidently the arguments which favoured an elderly bishop's designation of his successor to avert faction and to preserve capital endowments intact were not contemptsible. Valerius's problem was to persuade his episcopal colleagues to agree to such a pre-emptive move, and here much turned on the view of the primate who would be principal consecrator. Except for the proconsular province of which Carthage was metropolis, the churches in the North African provinces had a system of primatial leadership which gave the position to whichever bishop was senior by date of consecration, a system which always put very old men into the chair. (On one occasion two bishops of extreme senectitude both supposed themselves to have the senior position, and Augustine had to suggest to them that they sort out the confusion them-selves, please, before sending out rival summons to councils.) The senior bishop of Numidia, the province in which Hippo Regius was located, was at that time Megalius, of nearby Calama. Just as there was about to be an assembly of Numidian bishops gathered at Hippo for some celebration, perhaps a church dedication, Valerius revealed his wish to Megalius.

The primate had heard reports about Augustine that he did not like. His initial reaction was to write an intemperate letter to Valerius rejecting the proposal out of hand. Augustine had tried to help a distressed woman whose marriage was on the rocks by sending her some blessed bread. The slander had soon circulated that what Augustine sent her was a love-charm to assist her in her adulterous love, and that her husband connived at the whole thing. There had already been open criticism among the bishops of Valerius' unheard-of innovation, delegating to his presbyter teaching and preaching duties that elsewhere in Africa were the bishop's personal responsibility. Was his monastery really untouched by Manichaeism? Even if these questions were satisfactorily answered, there was strongly felt objection to conferring the episcopate on Augustine while Valerius was alive. On this point, however, precedents were discovered and quoted. Augustine was able to satisfy the bishops on the other matters. Valerius' people were evidently in full support of the plan. So Augustine became bishop. Within a few months, certainly by August 397, Valerius was dead, and Augustine was in sole charge of his diocese of Hippo city and its large hinterland extending many miles inland.

Although the African Catholic bishops had heard of the council of Nicaea (325) and rejected Arianism (below, pp. 118–19), no one at the time, or for more than twenty years afterwards, knew that the eighth canon of the council of Nicaea expressly forbade more than one bishop in one city.

Augustine could answer the objections made against his conduct as a presbyter. But he retained a sense of an unhealed shame about his pre-baptismal past, a sense which may have been stirred if Adeodatus' mother made any attempt to renew contact with him at the time of the boy's death. There is no evidence that in 396 anyone other than Augustine himself had qualms on this ground. Valerius' motive for wanting Augustine to succeed him is to be looked for in the need of the Catholics at Hippo to be led by a powerful orator who could justify and defend their position over against the overwhelming Donatist majority in the city. Augustine would put the Church on the map, as it can hardly have been under a man with unfluent Latin and many absences in South Italy.

Congregations normally expected their bishop not only to get them to heaven by his teaching but also to care for their worldly interests by squaring the secular authorities at government house or the tax office or the lawcourts. Augustine was not born into the senatorial class, and found such duties burdensome and sometimes very humiliating. His little flock, he says, watch with ignorant envy when he calls on secular potentates. They do not know how he has hated going, how he is 'kept waiting and waiting in the anterooms while worthy and unworthy persons are admitted first', and then when he is finally announced how reluctant the official is to grant an interview, how he may be humiliated, how often he is sent away sad (S 302. 17).

These words admittedly belong to the year 400 when the Catholic community in Hippo is still the merest handful, so that he could hardly claim to speak for any large body in the town, such as might command more respect in high places.

In the light of such experiences Augustine came to make it a principle in all negotiation, or in any controversy whatever, however wide the gulf may be that is to be bridged, that the other party must be treated as a partner in a shared discussion of a common problem and always, unless there is hard evidence to the contrary, as a man of good will and integrity. There was one practice normally expected of bishops which he declined to perform, namely to write references or letters of commendation to powerful patrons to fix appointments for people. He liked to quote in self-defence the ironic aphorism 'I have too much care for my own reputation to vouch for that of my friends' (Possidius, *Vita Augustini* 20).

Becoming a bishop meant that he could no longer live so austere and monastic a life. 'A bishop who failed to offer hospitality would be thought inhuman' (*S* 355. 2). (He did not make the mistake John Chrysostom made a year or so later at Constantinople in failing to entertain those who expected it of him.) He now controlled a church chest with twenty times the resources of his father's estate. Some thought he now ought to live with a comfort that would tell the world in the forum at Hippo that their bishop was an important personage. An attempt to give him a silk shirt or *byrrhus* met the firm reply: 'suitable for a bishop but not for Augustine, a poor man of poor parents—for then people would say that by becoming a bishop I have costly clothes I would never have had at home or in my secular profession' (*S* 356. 13).

With the death of Valerius Augustine had to move from the garden monastery into the bishop's house. He decided to turn it into a clergy-house. The quality and dedication of the clergy would be improved if they were taken away from their families in distant lodgings and suburbs, and brought together to live a quasi-monastic life in community under Augustine's care. That would also make it needless for them to undertake the part-time manual work by which many of them were earning their daily bread. The Hippo clergy-house became a nursery of qualified clergy who could go out to become bishops elsewhere. So under

Augustine the house was lived in by about three presbyters and five deacons. He experienced acute difficulty in imposing the requirement that, like monks, they should bestow their personal property upon the church chest, especially since he thought it proper to assume that they had done so even after he suspected they had not. Moreover, other bishops gave him no support in making this demand. Augustine wanted to make residence in the clergy-house and the surrender of property to the church a condition of employment in the city churches. Near the end of his life it became known that a widowed presbyter Januarius had kept substantial property undisclosed and in his will assigned it to the church, thereby, however, disinheriting his daughter and son. Augustine was much upset. He refused to accept the legacy at all, and so brought fierce lay criticism on his head from those who thought a bishop had a prime duty to maximize the church's corporate resources, whatever the human consequences. The greater the number of poor on the Catholic church welfare roll, the stronger its power in rivalry to the schismatic Donatists. The row made Augustine restate his principles. All legacies to the church should be that portion which a testator would allocate if he had an additional child. The Church must not accept legacies on terms unfair to and resented by the children, likely to involve the chest in financial worries later. It was wholly against his policy to keep liquid assets. There was no substantial cash-float kept in a church safe. If anyone presented him with something valuable in kind, he sold it at once and gave the proceeds to the poor. He himself sought always to live as Christ's pauper. It is not surprising perhaps that some of his clergy found it all too exacting.

In 411 a devout and rich couple from Italy, Pinianus and Melania, fled from Rome to Africa. They came to Thagaste, whence

Alypius conducted them on to Hippo. In the church service the faithful, realizing Pinianus to be a millionaire, suddenly demanded that Augustine do as Valerius had done to him; he should ordain Pinianus. Tumult ensued. The ordination was averted only by Pinianus swearing that he would accept ordination neither at Hippo nor elsewhere—an oath offensive to Alypius who tried to prevent it and was painfully jostled by the crowd. Augustine defended his flock with noble charity, pleading that his people were surely in search of pure goodness of character, not in the least out for money to finance love-feasts and more poor on the church roll.

Women were not admitted to stay at the clergy house. Even his sister and his brother's daughters, who also became nuns, would not come to visit him 'lest false rumours spread among the uninformed or the weak be upset'. Augustine once remarks that for anyone in a very public position it is not enough to have a clear conscience and ignore the damage done by malicious misrepresentation. An aristocratic monk being pressed by his mother to forsake his monastery is sharply told: 'Guard against the Eve in every woman, even your mother' (*E* 243. 10). Possidius tells us that Augustine was always careful, but entirely ready to give a woman a private spiritual consultation if she had some personal matter to unburden.

# 6

# NORTH AFRICAN CHRISTIANITY

THE North African churches could look back with proper pride on heroic figures of the past. Tertullian's deviation into Montanist pentecostalism had only little diminished the admiration commanded by his writings, though Augustine read him with reserve and thought his considerable wit too raw and unrefined. The supreme hero remained Cyprian, martyred in 258. Devout souls like Monnica would go and spend the night in his shrine by the harbour at Carthage to ask his protection and care (*C* 5. 8. 15). The anniversary of his martyrdom or *natalis* ('birthday') on 14 September was a great event in the Christian year. During the persecution of Diocletian (303–5) the African churches suffered a furnace of trial, which not only produced long-lasting division among the Christians, but also added martyrs to the church's roll of honour in the calendar. Hippo on 15 November remembered its 220 martyrs. Naturally the main feasts of the calendar were those already familiar in the Church—Easter, Ascension, Pentecost, Christmas; Lent (but not yet Advent). Some feasts were established to wean the people from pagan rites, e.g. St John Baptist on 24 June to keep the Africans from a ceremonial bathe and midsummer bonfires. On

1 January the Christians fasted in penitential protest against the pagan feasting which consumed much liquor.

At the annual commemorations of martyrs Christians went to their shrines for a celebration of the liturgy, and would bring wine and food, just as their pagan ancestors had done to appease the shades of the departed. They liked holy pictures as talismans (*ME* I. 34. 75). They used the ancient and highly edifying sign of the cross as if it were magic rather than a recall to compunction of heart.

Augustine felt that a reform such as Ambrose had successfully carried through at Milan was needed in North Africa. One of his earliest letters to Bishop Valerius, during his presbyterate, observes that the intoxicating celebrations on saints' days might have some chance of reformation if the clergy ceased to accept a personal offering for celebrating the liturgy, and preached more sermons with scriptural explanations so that the people had a clearer understanding. The people are right to believe that the sacrifice of their Lord on the cross atones for the sins of the whole Church, living and departed, and that the eucharist, in which the Church offers itself as the body of Christ, is an intercession and pleading of Christ's merits. But superstition may obscure this truth, and is fatally encouraged by the payment of requiem fees to the clergy and by drinking on saints' days. Augustine drily remarks that of the three faults censured by the apostle in Rom. 13: 13–14, drunkenness, sexual licence, and contentiousness, only the second seemed to be taken seriously by the African churches. There was general toleration, unparalleled in Italy, of the scenes of popular inebriation among the laity on feast days, while the episcopate lost credit not merely by individual bishops seeking consolation in the bottle but also by the public acrimony with which they strove against each other and by the compulsive desire of some for the limelight. Augustine placed an inscription on his hospitable dinner-table forbidding malicious gossip. Once a group of fellow-bishops transgressed the rule; he sharply declared that he would retire from the meal if the catty talk continued. Wine in strict restraint he thought good, but excess in food or drink hateful: 'The banquet which the rich man in Christ's parable ate on earth he digested in hell' (*EP* 48. 2. 8).

The progress of the Christian mission and the decline of paganism were increasingly visible in the last decades of the fourth century. The temples were becoming empty, and were soon to be dismantled by order of imperial authority. Theodosius I issued edicts forbidding pagan sacrifice on pain of death. Were not God's fishermen, the apostles, now gaining the emperor and, more gradually, the senate as well? Until the fourth century the Christian mission in the West had not gone far with the barbarian tribes beyond the line of frontier forts. Augustine knew churches had long been established in Persia and India; but nearer home, to the south of the North African coastal strip, there were unevangelized tribesmen in remote hill-country and on the edge of the desert. In Augustine's time there was a great stirring among some of these tribesmen, coming down to the Numidian cities and asking to be instructed in the Christian faith. In the Roman cities of Africa churches were well attended. Augustine tells one crowded Easter congregation how happy he is to see them, and how much happier he would be if he did not also know that the same crowd would next day be at the amphitheatre watching a bloody gladiatorial show. Attendance was particularly high at great festivals like Easter, Pentecost, and Christmas, but could be thin at other times of the year. One sermon preached as part of a

Lenten course at a town near Hippo complains that the church is half-empty because so many are at the local music-hall—a place to which lukewarm Christians flock, but 'where they would be shocked to see their clergy' (*SDen* 17. 8–9). However, one should not be put off by hypocrites, who are to be found in every profession. In Africa you may have to go far to find even one church where no one has been discovered in crime and where no clergy have had to be degraded (*CLP* 3. 31. 36). Too many come to church for non-religious reasons, to please a powerful patron, to win a wife, to escape some failure in their secular career, or even in search of physical health. Augustine does not wish to drive them away, for many who first come for worldly reasons (as indeed he had done himself), may discover an authentic faith in time. 'A convert will find many good Christians in the Church if he sets out to become one himself' (*CR* 7. 11).

Augustine feared that his congregation might be too concerned for its own consolations and insufficiently outward-looking. To an unbeliever their attitude ought to be one of love, not hostility, so that he may actually come to want to become a brother (*EJ* 1. 11). 'How many of Christ's enemies at the present day are being suddenly drawn by a secret grace?' (*IIepPel* 1. 19. 37). Augustine's psychological interest leads him to notice how the patience, faith, and charity of converted harlots and popular entertainers can utterly surpass that of conventional Christians. At the beginning of the ninth book of the *Confessions* he is puzzled that the turning of the will occurs in a single moment, and yet is a moment in a long movement over many years; he wonders how it comes about that it can suddenly be delightful to be without the 'sweet trivialities' that were once indispensable to him. Augustine never thinks it a sensible question to ask what causes a choice made by the free will (*CD* 12. 6; *LA* 2. 20. 54, 3. 17. 48). In the first book of the *Soliloquies* he writes that the proper way to examine a decision is to inquire into its consequential effects. 'Love is the weight by which I act' (*C* 13. 9. 10). 'We come near to God not by walking, but by loving' (*non ambulando, sed amando*: *E* 155. 4. 13).

Augustine's favourite pictures of the Church are in the parables of the kingdom in Matthew 13. The field contains both wheat and tares, without uprooting the tares before the final harvest. How can the Church remain holy if it is bound to tolerate scandals such as sinners 'who are in communion with the Church's sacraments but not with the Church' (*U* 25. 74)? The puritan Donatists thought that the principle of regretful toleration meant the destruction of discipline and the practical abolition of the New Testament practice of excommunication. Augustine is much more flexible about individuals than about churches and canon law and institutional structures. (He cannot be said to have had much interest in canon law and institutional structures at any time.) He felt that excommunication must be rarely employed, and never when its use may merely drive the person under discipline into a schismatic or heretical group.

Some African bishops received requests for baptism from candidates whose present spouse was their second, while the first, divorced spouse was still alive and perhaps remarried. Could Catholic baptism wash away all the past and, thereby validate the existing marriage as that which God recognizes? If we may not quite say this, may such candidates be now baptized without more ado and then, afterwards, gradually learn that the discipline of holiness requires them to acknowledge only their first marriage to be valid before God, even though that acknowledgement will entail painful consequences; no doubt their second marriage may in the circumstances be treated as a venial sin. This liberal approach of his African colleagues seemed to Augustine too dangerous (FO). It would lay the Catholic bishops open to charges of abandoning any discipline at all: it is better to be thought to be standing for something on principle than to appear to allow anything.

St Paul had told the Corinthians not to take grievances against one another before secular lawcourts. Disagreements within the community should be settled by arbitration. Such cases occupied quantities of episcopal time. Augustine found that most of those who brought cases before the bishop's court were not good and loyal believers but members with a long record of being contentious. He did not find the role of arbitrator easy. One quickly becomes the object of slander if, as is frequently the case, the controversy is between rich and poor. To decide for the rich man is to invite accusations of toadying to the powerful—who, to Augustine's anger, expected the Church to play the part of keeping the poor quiet. To decide for the weak man is to invite accusations of bribery. Augustine found that in cases where the rich man had justice on his side, the bishop should unhesitatingly decide in his favour, but should then ask him to show mercy (EP 32. 2. 12). Augustine found such cases very complex because, as he put it, the necessities of the poor are the superfluities of the rich, the luxuries of the poor are the necessities of the rich (EP 147. 12; Regula ad servos Dei 3. 4).

Debtors, runaway slaves, those oppressed by the tax-men, and criminals on the run, might seek asylum at the altar. A steep rise in interest rates during the 390s had driven many into bankruptcy; Jerome thought it a leading cause of rioting in several cities of the empire as bankruptcy generated unemployment. Augustine sometimes had to pay a large sum to keep a debtor out of prison, and would then send the collection-bag round the congregation asking them to meet the cost (*E* 268). He much admired a bishop of Thagaste before Constantine's time who hid a refugee from justice: when summoned himself for interrogation, he won pardon for himself and the delinquent by replying that with him it was a moral principle neither to tell a lie nor to betray a man (*M* 13. 23).

Augustine regretted but did not refuse the social and secular function a bishop was expected to perform, though he constantly called it 'the bishop's burden'. It was a pity that so many 'run to the church not for eternal life but for temporal aid', and then complain that only old women and widows filled the churches.

The experience of doing the work of a bishop made far deeper and more obvious changes in Augustine's character than even his conversion at Milan ten years before. He rapidly shed the tone of a dilettante eclectic picking out what he liked in Christianity and in Platonism. Shouldering the initially highly unwelcome responsibilities turned him into a great man such as he would never have become had he remained a professor of rhetoric. All the masterpieces on which later centuries looked back were without exception written during his busy life as bishop, not while he was a leisured young 'don'. Until his ordination as presbyter in 391, his ideal had been that of a Platonic elite within the Church, preserving contemplative detachment far from getting and spending, the sweat and toil of the peasants on the vast African estates, or matrimonial squabbles and petty ambitions. His elite of cultured people engaged in plain living and high thinking did not need aids to their senses like relics or material miracles to bring them reminders of the supernatural. By taking orders, or rather having them thrust upon him (his letters make it clear that this was in Africa a frequent pattern, of which he was not the only victim), he had to identify himself with an essentially populist body with a more or less complete cross-section of society from dukes to dustmen, held together in equality before God and his law; a realm in which the rich man's wealth can buy nothing worth having.

Already in 390 while he was still a layman, the change of attitude is foreshadowed in an exchange of letters between Augustine and a pagan professor of grammar at nearby Madauros, named Maximus. Augustine invited him to consider becoming a Christian. Maximus ironically refused: Under different forms are not all religions ultimately one and the same? Polytheism happens to suit me, as Christianity suits you; each to his personal taste. In any event, I prefer Roman Jupiter and Juno to the martyrs with uncouth Punic names venerated by the Numidian churches.

Augustine's rejoinder is a grave rebuke for Maximus' elegant scepticism and poseur-like manner. Above all Augustine rejects his scorn for Punic-speaking martyrs who in conscientious integrity died for their beliefs. Religion is for him a far stronger bond than class or culture. The same attitude appears in one of his most excited sermons at Hippo telling his congregation about the movement among the remote tribesmen coming down from the hills to knock at the bishop's door. 'And what do you want? To know the glory of God' (*EP* 134. 22). The Church and the Empire are not coterminous. Barbarians beyond the frontier are to come in also.

Slowly but surely Augustine identifies himself with the devotions of his people. He never despises their longing for supernatural signs of divine presence. At Milan in June 386, at the height of the troubles between Ambrose and the Arian empress Justina demanding the surrender of basilicas for her fellow Arians the Goths, the remains of two Milanese saints Gervasius and Protasius were found and then conducted in procession to the cathedral. Wild enthusiasm was generated when a blind man's sight was restored with a handkerchief that had touched the holy relics. Augustine was not an eye-witness, though in Milan at the time, and the event had no influence on his conversion. He mentions it only later as an afterthought in the ninth book of the *Confessions*. In 390 in the essay *On True Religion* he says that miracles occurred in apostolic times when the Church was starting out, but do not happen now. 'If we look for a cause of awe and wonder now, we should contemplate nature' (*UC* 16. 34). 'The daily miracles of creation are as great as those of the incarnate Lord' (*TJ* 9. 1). A sermon of 400 declares that miracles of inward moral conversion are greater than the material miracles once done by Christ himself: now the Lord opens not blind eyes but blind hearts. The present continuation of the miracles of the apostolic age is to be found in the sacraments of the Church.

A shift from this position is first to be seen with Paulinus of Nola's correspondence from Italy assuring him that by the shrine of St Felix sick folk are being healed and perjurers unmasked. In 404 Augustine writes in puzzlement that in Africa, despite its many shrines, such wonders do not happen. A quarrel broke out between a Hippo monk and one of Augustine's presbyters, their stories being incompatible so that one must be lying. Augustine, though virtually certain the presbyter was telling the truth, could not feel quite sure, and therefore sent both to Nola to swear before St Felix.

The rival Donatist community jubilantly claimed miracles at their own *martyria*. At the tomb of Donatus himself, humble Donatist prayers were answered, and oaths were sworn 'by his grey hairs'. The Catholic community might find it hard to allow their schismatic rivals to trump them. In a sermon of about 410 Augustine notes that 'cures by the merit of the martyrs are becoming more frequent now' (*EP* 118. 30. 5).

In December 415 relics of St Stephen, the first martyr, were discovered at Caphargamala near Jerusalem, and through a Greek priest named Lucian some part of this treasure was acquired by a presbyter of Braga (now in Portugal), who intended Orosius to take the holy objects to his home church. The Germanic invasions of the Iberian peninsula frustrated the plan, and the relics ended by being divided between Ancona, Minorca, and Uzalis in North Africa. Reports of healings began to come in.

By 426 when he is writing the last book of the *City of God* Augustine wants his pagan readers to realize that at the tombs of the saints miracles now happen, 'not such notable wonders as in apostolic days, but not none at all' (*R* 1. 14. 5). Even then, however, he disallows any claim that they vindicate Christianity against paganism or Catholicism against sects. Charity is more important than miracles (*TJ* 17. 1). In 412 he writes that 'that faith is stronger which needs no recourse to miracles' (*PM* 2. 32. 52); they belong in the Church's infancy. Evil powers and schismatics produce miracles. We do not believe in the Church because of miracles; if and when we are disposed to accept that a miracle has occurred, that is because we believe in the Church. And if miracles are granted, that is a sign that we are still immature. Augustine is in principle expressly unsympathetic to those whose religion turns on the veneration of saints or angels, since they may look more for miracles than for the moral example of the saints' devotion to God (*T* 8. 7. 11), and try to live the life of faith by sight (*PM* 2. 32. 52).

Augustine never concedes that miracles can be 'contrary to nature'. 'Nothing intrinsically impossible falls within divine omnipotence' (*F* 26. 3–5). God has given both laws of nature and also hidden potentialities of growth in the creative seeds he originally implanted. So both vitality and form are signs of God's immanent presence to the natural environment. At the same time God remains a superior cause. 'God does nothing contrary to nature; a miracle is contrary only to what our minds expect, but God never acts against the supreme law of nature any more than he acts against himself.'

Unbelievers mock Christian belief in the Virgin Birth and the Resurrection of Christ, not seeing the special care a universal providence may take for human need. These are signs that show Christ to be a unique person. Augustine would therefore much dislike rationalists who defend the Virgin Birth with instances of parthenogenesis among animals, because that would wholly miss the point (*E* 102. 4).

# 7

# CHRISTIAN CULTURE

## Questions for Simplician

I N the first years after he had become a bishop Augustine wrote three important books: the *Questions for Simplician*, the first three (of four) books *On Christian Teaching*, and the *Confessions*.

Simplician at Milan had influenced Augustine in the months before his conversion. He soon wrote to congratulate Augustine on his elevation at Hippo, and perhaps also to communicate his own election as Ambrose's successor in April 397. Simplician coupled his felicitations with a request for help with the interpretation of Paul's epistle to the Romans and some queries from the Old Testament. To support their dualism the Manichees appealed to Romans 7, with Paul's agonized portrait of man's moral conflict torn between conscience and impulse, knowing the right and the good but lacking sufficient will to do it. For their determinism Manichees appealed to the apostle's discussion of predestination in Romans 9. In the last third of the fourth century in the Latin West the exegesis of St Paul became an increasingly lively issue. The epistles received systematic commentaries from Marius Victorinus, from a highly intelligent anonymous commentator in the 370s at Rome (called by scholars Ambrosiaster, his work having been transmitted under Ambrose's name); then about 400 from Pelagius, a British monk lately settled in Rome who feared Manichaeism like a blight.

In 397 replying to Simplician, Augustine writes the first overture to a coming drama. He takes Romans 7 to portray man under law before God's grace has transformed his moral will. (Twenty years later the Pelagian controversy will force him to abandon this view.) Romans 9 is taken in 397 to mean that faith and a good will are both God's gifts. Why does God give them to some and not to others? We can say only that his justice is inscrutable, and that if, among his many debtors, a creditor decides to remit the debts of some and not others, he has the right to do so. Those from whom payment of their dues is exacted have no conceivable ground for complaint against the justice of the action. The Manichees saw Jacob and Esau as prefiguring the elect and the damned, who are, in Manichee belief, what they are by nature through divine decree. Augustine is moved by his text to concede that indeed they prefigure the saved and the lost. But these are what they are by will, not by nature which is created good. Granted, the good will of the elect is God's gift; yet because his grace is sovereign, there can be no arguing with our Maker.

In short, Augustine no longer believes, as he once did, that there is an identifiable area in human action which belongs exclusively to individual, personal choice. Grace gives all, since without it the will, though free, lacks the power to do good. Grace and freedom are not like independent entities cooperating in mutual respect for each other's autonomy. Free choice can do what is good only insofar as it is penetrated by grace in the core of a man's being.

## Christian Education

A result of Augustine's ordination to the presbyterate and then to the episcopate was a great increase in his concern to understand the Bible. Late in 396 or early in 397 he began a treatise On Christian Teaching (*De doctrina christiana*), which was first published thirty years later when he completed the last third of the work. Its subject is how to teach Christianity, not a general handbook to education. The work came to be hugely influential in medieval times and was the first book by Augustine to be printed. Augustine's starting-point is that while the content of what Christians have to teach is a divine word, yet the problem of the right way to teach it is no different from that of teaching any department of human knowledge.

Because the Christian teacher is expounding a God-given record in Scripture, he must not imagine that he can rely exclusively on direct inspiration to tell him what it all means. He needs to ask questions such as how language communicates truth, and how language about God can be meaningfully used when it must be even more inadequate to its object than all language is. A good Biblical interpreter needs training in a variety of disciplines. First comes grammar or the laws of language. Since the Latin Bible is a translation (and one done by people of more virtue than knowledge), Christian studies should include Greek and Hebrew. Unlike Jerome, Augustine himself knew no Hebrew. But he knew very well that the New Testament includes transliterated Hebrew words like Raca, Hosanna, Alleluia, or Amen; and Hebrew proper names have special meanings which the interpreter must attend to. Augustine's exegetical writings often refer to the Greek texts. He would no doubt have wished to study Hebrew had he not believed that the Greek version of the Seventy (Septuagint) commissioned by King Ptolemy I is no less divinely given than the Hebrew original. He often refers to variants between the manuscripts. Augustine had first begun his Bible studies in Italy, and thought that the type of text current in Italy was superior to the more careless African manuscripts.

Next the interpreter needs some knowledge of chronology so as to relate the Biblical history to the dates of Greek and Roman history, Olympiads and consulships: e.g. Ambrose had made a great impression by his argument that Jeremiah and Plato lived in the same century and therefore could easily have met and conversed in Egypt. Then there are other subjects on the frontiers of the Biblical interpreter's work, especially geography and natural history to help with the places, animals, trees, plants, and minerals mentioned in the Bible. 'Even technology is useful if it enables one to see the point of a simile.' The pagan study of natural science includes astrology and magical beliefs, so that the Christian will be careful in this department of knowledge. But logic is wholly indispensable: the truth of valid inference is no merely human invention but a discovering of divinely given fact. It belongs to the objective order of things that if a consequent is false, the antecedent will also be false. The four mathematical disciplines are arithmetic, music, geometry, and astronomy. In the ancient Platonic and Pythagorean tradition numbers become clues to the structure of the cosmos, and the very order and mutual relation of the planets is determined by musical ratios. Because in Scripture numbers can be obviously symbolic (e.g. 'forty days and forty nights') Augustine, in common with many ancient exegetes, deduces that all Biblical numbers are clues to the inner meaning. The discussions of Plato and the classical philosophers are to be used by the Christian interpreter in the spirit of the ancient Hebrews who, at the Exodus, 'spoiled the Egyptians' by borrowing their jewellery.

Since this course of preparatory study is enormous, Augustine thinks the interpreter has the right to aids. Otherwise he will spend much time on the detailed study of subjects where he needs only a little to illuminate his problem. It is therefore his hope that some diligent persons may compile lists of place-names, birds, beasts, plants, and metals in the Bible. What is needed is a Bible dictionary. Augustine's remarks on this subject helped to bring into existence the type of learned reference book which we now think of as an encyclopaedia.

The well-prepared interpreter now faces a grander question, namely the actual principles of interpretation. The Bible contains a wide diversity of books (though 'some call the canonical scriptures one book because of their divine unity', *EP* 150. 2), and at first sight much is ambiguous and obscure. The Christian community's tradition in the creed and 'rule of faith' is a sound criterion where Scripture speaks with an ambiguous voice on essential doctrine. But the Biblical writers employ much allegory and symbolism, so that it can be a delicate matter to determine what is literal and what is figurative, or where an apparent absurdity shows that a literal sense cannot be intended, or how kernel and husk are to be distinguished. If anyone thinks providence neglectful in allowing obscurities into Scripture, he should reflect on the psychological fact that human beings appreciate little what has cost them little. (Augustine first articulates the proposition that 'value' is a function of the labour that has gone into a thing's making.)

In his quest for rules of interpretation, for the avoidance of mere subjectivity, Augustine is influenced by Ticonius, a dissident Donatist of a generation previously, censured by his own cloth for conceding to the Catholic opposition that the true Church must be universal rather than defined as 'what someone happens to think holy'. About 380 he wrote an extant book of seven *Rules or Keys* to unlock the obscurities of the Bible, which Augustine, across the dust and blood of ecclesiastical polemics, recognized to be a work of insight and intelligence. No small part of Ticonius' system of theology became incorporated into the thinking behind Augustine's *City of God*.

The fourth and last book on Christian teaching asks what place eloquence may properly have in presenting religious truth. In late antiquity secular oratory became ornate and therefore loved obscurity; it tended to be the art of saying next to nothing beautifully. Those who mastered rhetoric in the schools might hope for some public career in the civil service or, if not that, for a teaching position from which they could perpetuate the tradition. Apart from the lawcourts, public oratory on great occasions in secular life was almost confined to imperial panegyrics, a genre of which Augustine, himself the author of one, had a low opinion. In his *Soliloquies* he pays a compliment to an unnamed member of the Cassiciacum–Milan circle 'in whom we see eloquence, which we had thought dead, come to life again' (*Solil.* 2. 14. 26). The reference is probably not to Ambrose. Nevertheless, the place of the sermon in Christian worship gave a new impulse to the art of oratory. Augustine felt that eloquence was less necessary to clergy than the basic discipline of Bible study; but they could learn useful lessons by attending, if not to the detailed prescriptions, at least to the broad principles laid down by Cicero in his *Orator*. In itself oratory is morally neither good nor bad; it is damnable when used to persuade people to accept error. Unlike Cicero, Augustine does not say rhetoric is an art indispensable to every educated man. He emphatically denies that every educated Christian should study its methods at any cost. But oratory is not to be rejected. Ciceronian eloquence has three aims: to instruct, to please, to move, and has three styles for doing this—simple, or florid, or pathetic. The Christian orator alters the order of priorities; it is more important to instruct and to move, and only lastly to please. Elaborate language and convoluted sentences will defeat the object, and therefore a Christian teacher should use direct speech, and take the Bible as a model for form as well as the source of his content.

Augustine's programme is concerned with religious instruction, not with education generally; scientific knowledge is marginal to the scheme. In the *Confessions* (5. 4. 7) he remarks that one who knows God has found happiness even if ignorant of astronomy. But Augustine has no fear of the natural sciences. Rather his fear is of theologians, orthodox in intention, who try to treat the book of Genesis as a source-book for science without realizing the very different purpose of the sacred book. Like Mani, they merely end in writing bad science and bring discredit on their faith. By pursuing science our minds may grasp everything in heaven and earth, but still remain baffled at the problem of human nature and destiny (*AO* 4. 6. 7–9. 13). Augustine wants a middle road between credulity, which is asking too few questions, and 'curiosity' which is asking too many (*UC* 9. 22–11. 25).

The completion of Augustine's statement of his educational programme was deferred until near the end of his life, as if he then had a presentiment of the imminent Vandal conquest and of the coming general collapse of the Roman educational system under the barbarian invasions. During his last years he became consciously concerned 'to write for future generations', and obtained from his people at Hippo their signed and sealed agreement (which of course was not kept) to allow him several days a week free of interruptions. Before his death on 30 August 430 during the Vandal siege of Hippo, his last command was 'See that the church library and all the books are carefully preserved for posterity.'

Rightly enough, he realized that the probability of survival was small, and that a library is a profitable tool only if there are people who know how to use it. The survival of so large a part of Augustine's works (the amount lost is relatively small) shows that his instruction was carried out.

The treatise *On Christian Teaching* presupposes, however, that the Roman educational system will continue. After its collapse men like Cassiodorus, in a sixth-century Italy ravaged by drunken Goths and then a terrible twenty years of Byzantine reconquest, looked to Augustine's book as a charter for building an educational pattern for which no body except the Church could now be responsible. In consequence the limitations of horizon chosen by Augustine for his specific purpose will come to define the areas in which medieval schools work. Contrary to his intention, Augustine was taken to be writing an agreed syllabus for the schools of Christian times.

'Educated Christians like myself', he wrote to Simplician (*DS* 1. 2. 22), 'expect God's grace to prefer people of greater natural ability, higher standards of behaviour, and superior education in the liberal arts. In fact God mocks my expectations.' The

Church teacher works in a comprehensive school in which there is no segregation of pupils of high ability. Among those receiving instruction are manual workers and peasants who maintain the state of the world by labour which is also their prayer, but do not read books. How can they receive instruction? For a sophisticated deacon of Carthage named Deogratias, who found difficulty in his classes of instruction, Augustine wrote an absorbing and delightful little treatise *On Catechizing Simple People* (*De catechizandis rudibus*). Admittedly the recipients of the proposed instruction are not all naïve folk who suppose, when they hear that the risen Christ 'sits at the right hand of the Father', that the Father must be sitting on Christ's left. Augustine's main concern is with the method of instructing people having some modest secondary but no higher education, inclined to laugh at ignorant bishops (a favourite butt of the half-educated, Augustine observes), sadly vulnerable to superstitions, divination, amulets, and astrology, incapable of sufficient concentration to listen to anything but a brief discourse, yet able to grasp a straightforward idea when directly presented to them.

In his own preaching Augustine does not speak the demotic Latin of the streets, but is careful to avoid long sermons with complex sentences. Nothing is said indirectly or ironically, or to entertain. His eyes are not on his script or notes if any, but on his hearer's faces, and he is ready to stop or to shift the direction of his discourse immediately if he is losing their attention. A natural cheerfulness is a quality indispensable to an effective teacher, he remarks. The congregation will enjoy (and rightly) a well-understood sermon; indeed the more so if it leads them to tears of penitence and obedience to the Biblical text being expounded. Ciceronian prose being deeply in his blood,

Augustine's sermons contain the occasional antithesis or rhyming Latin, provided it comes naturally. His directness to his flock is a consciously adopted simplicity which knows just what effect monosyllables may achieve. Even the simplest thing is somehow said in a way that is fresh and conducive to reflection.

## *The* Confessions

In 397–8 the manuscript on Christian teaching was pushed aside unfinished in favour of a greater enterprise. His continued writings against the Manichees had set out to refute their interpretation of Genesis and of St Paul, and his mind battled away with the grand questions of Platonic metaphysics in relation to Christian faith. This mixture of themes was filling his mind when about the spring of 397 there arrived for him and for Alypius twin letters from the great aristocrat Paulinus, who in 395 had turned his back on a career of the highest secular eminence to settle in Italy at Nola (Campania) where he wished to build churches and hospices for pilgrims at the shrine of his favourite saint and benefactor St Felix. At Nola Paulinus founded a monastic community, news of which reached Thagaste. Monasteries founded by millionaires not being then an everyday occurrence, Alypius wrote him a letter of fraternal greeting. Paulinus had never met Augustine or Alypius, but was glad to return greetings from beyond the seas from brothers who, unlike many in Italy and elsewhere, had expressed no misgivings about his abandonment of secular responsibilities. Paulinus was not a little fascinated by the drama of his own career, since his renunciation had been a matter of some éclat throughout the West, and asked Alypius to send him details of his personal autobiography.

This request inspired Augustine into writing his supreme masterpiece, the *Confessions*. The book is very unlike anything else he wrote except the early *Soliloquies*. By a unique mixture he not merely expounds his Platonizing solution of evil as non-being or the absence of good with a rejection of Manichee exposition of Genesis and St Paul, but also sets out a doctrine of divine grace and human destiny. To this last theme his autobiography is presented as a subordinate illustration. The autobiography had the merit of answering critics anxious about his Manichee past; to his surprise a large number of people, not all friendly, seemed to be curious about his life-history. Since his months at Cassiciacum he had made private meditation his daily practice, and together with his brothers at Thagaste and Hippo had recited or chanted the Psalter. In the *Confessions* he adopts the extraordinary form of a prose-poem addressed to his Maker, not to human readers. The content of the work turns upon the double meaning of *confessio* as both praise and the admission of faults. In the manner of its presentation of ideas the work is the peak of which his preceding writings are like ascending foothills and soaring ridges. If the *Confessions* climb higher still, that is because the vehement love of Augustine's passionate nature is now directed to God in adoration and mystical union.

The literary structure of the *Confessions* is loose and often unclear. Augustine himself is aware of his tendency to be discursive and, at one point, begs the Lord to help him to keep to the point. The encyclopaedia of his mind is full of questions, and he wanders into bypaths at the least provocation. The last three books are a Neoplatonizing commentary on the first chapter of Genesis and often show striking affinities with ideas found in the third-century Greek theologian Origen. In these books 'confession' means praise rather than penitence. Although hurried readers often pass by these books unread because of their lack of autobiographical matter, they also contain essential clues to the thought of the work as a whole.

The central theme of the *Confessions* is the alienation of man from his true self. The soul that has lost God has lost its roots and therefore has lost itself. For the soul is inherently unstable on its own. Because it is created out of nothing, it is mutable; vulnerable to a loss of coherence and unity, to being pulled in a hundred and one directions and so to becoming unable to see below the mere surface of things. Surrender to the tumult of passions renders the soul insensitive to the spiritual dimension which is the soul's true destiny. The soul that has become disordered bears a self-inflicted misery, 'tired of living, scared of dying' (*C* 4. 6, 11). The sin that we begin by choosing freely becomes the fettering necessity of unbreakable habit. The hunger that we seek to allay becomes insatiable desire. Man's very ambition to play God reveals his creatureliness. 'As I became more wretched, you drew nearer to me.' In God alone can happiness be found. 'You have made us for yourself, and our heart finds no rest until it rests in you.' So, at the beginning of the work, the theme of the whole is announced.

The fall of Adam is a neglect, a choosing of what is inferior, a turning towards the creaturely as if it could be a worthy object of adoration. The consequences have affected all his descendants. The innocence and natural goodness of childhood Augustine thinks an illusion. No being can be more grasping and self-centred than the baby in the cot. If infants do no harm, that is for lack of strength, not of will. But because man never wholly loses the image of God stamped on him by creation, damaged though it is, he is a divided self. This division within the self is not to be explained on the Manichee hypothesis that man originates in a pre-cosmic mix-up of light and darkness in conflict with one another. Among other reasons for rejecting it is the fact that our wills are seldom split between two simple choices, one good, the other evil, but can be torn apart in a dozen directions with traumatic and paralysing effect. Evil is an absence of good, as the Platonists say, not an ultimate 'nature' but a perversion of the will, so that even our best actions have some intermingling of self-interest which lies beyond our power to eradicate.

The corrosion of man's heart lies deep; yet the remedy of divine grace penetrates no less far. Augustine speaks of God as 'not only outside me but at the core of my being' (C 13. 8. 9). The specific content of Christianity is the affirmation, then, that God has not merely given a moral law with teachers and prophets, but has, in the Incarnation, become man. The sacrifice of Christ's atoning death is a supreme divine mercy, a cancelling of guilt and the penalty of sinfulness. Access to this redemption is through the proclamation and the sacraments entrusted to the apostolic community of Christ's people. The Church sets us as pilgrims on the road to the heavenly Jerusalem, the glorious city of God.

Augustine's story of his quest is all his own, and yet is simultaneously (and evidently consciously) intended to be a portrait of Everyman. The ship of his life ventures out into dangerous seas. His route to harbour is out of his own control, and he feels himself blown to his destination by a divine hurricane. For him the constraint of grace has ended in a monastic calling to give up marriage and to pursue continence. 'O Love ever burning, never quenched, Love my God, set me on fire. You command continence. Grant what you command, and command what you please' (C10. 29. 40).

Classical Greek and Latin moralists had often spoken as if the human problem consists in the accidental attachment to an originally pure reason of an embarrassing collection of emotions such as anger, pity, grief, joy, lust, etc. To liberate oneself from the pain these emotions cause, one must suppress them. Rationality is the supreme thing. Augustine is critical of this way of thinking, and his criticism marks an epoch in the history of human moral consciousness. The ancient moralists often give the impression that they expect a man so to cultivate cool reason as to become virtually incapable of being moved. Augustine knows, of course, that our emotions are disordered. But the feelings are not in themselves the cause of the disorder which has deeper roots. The most powerful constituents of human nature are the emotions. They do not need repressing, and insensibility is impossible anyway. The setting apart of reason and emotion is inherently foolish. The emotions need not repression but elevation and purification, which are found as man's being is directed upwards towards his true destiny in faith and obedience. Only the Creator gives shape and order to chaos, whether in the cosmos or in our souls. The commentators on Genesis in Augustine's time debated whether the 'spirit' moving above the face of the waters is the Holy Spirit tranquilly ordering things, or a part of the turbulent world that needs to be ordered; in other words a hurricane. Augustine much prefers the former view. In God love is an ordered thing, a doctrine which Augustine (*CD* 15. 22) probably found in Origen's commentary on the Song of Songs. In one sermon (*S* 159. 2. 2) he tells his people 'Among all that gives you delight, let what is right be the supreme source of pleasure; not that other things do not give you delight, but that righteousness gives more delight. Some things naturally give pleasure to our infirmity, as food and drink give pleasure to the hungry and thirsty. Likewise we experience delight in the light of the rising sun, or of the moon and stars, or even earthly lights that lighten our darkness on earth. We derive pleasure from a musical voice and a sweet song or an agreeable odour. Our sense of touch is delighted by sexual pleasure . . . which is lawful with your spouse but unlawful with a harlot.' But Augustine (following a sermon of Origen available to him in Latin) then takes the five senses as symbols of the spiritual contact of the soul with God.

The publication of the *Confessions*, probably 398–400, divided Augustine's readers. In 427 Augustine looked back on them with the words: 'The *Confessions* enkindle the mind and feelings of man towards God. At least so far as I myself am concerned, they have had this effect on me when I have begun to reread them. What others think is for them to say. But I know that they have pleased and still do please a great number of brothers' (*R* 2. 6. 1). A faint touch of self-defence can be discerned here. There were other readers who read the book as an implicit admission that, despite all his disavowals, the old Manichee dualism was still only superficially purged away. In Africa Augustine's opponents, especially among the Donatists, pruriently exploited the narrative of his pre-baptismal surrender to sensuality and unkindly suggested that in such matters he had some way to go still, or, more ironically, that it was no doubt all right for someone who had had so much youthful sex to be now teaching the world chastity. But it is perhaps significant that there is no hint of any attempt by Augustine's enemies to extract revelations from his former girlfriend; perhaps by the time of the publication of the *Confessions* she was no longer alive—but if alive, she gave away nothing.

The ancient readers could not fail to notice that this ex-professor of rhetoric, who described his conversion as a renunciation of the secularity of empty eloquence, never composed a more wonderful piece of prose than this. The high climaxes of his religious experience are described with a wealth of overtones and with literary and philosophical allusions that are deliberate. For a description of the brutalizing effect of a gladiatorial combat on the spectators in an amphitheatre, no narrative in ancient literature begins to compare with C 6. 8. 13. Can such supreme artistry, the reader then and now must ask, be reconciled with the spontaneous sincerity we expect of those who lay bare their soul? Men fear truth presented to them in exquisite language (C 5. 6. 10).

It is sufficient reply that Augustine is using his mastery of language not to evoke admiration but for a religious end. The religious content of the book is never the means to achieve the end of an exquisite style or the applause of his readers. Moreover, the Confessions are shot through with quotations and echoes of the Psalms. The links between successive books are often provided by identical texts from the Psalter, and the psalm-citations have been shown to be integral to the literary structure of the work. Augustine is never a puritan, and sees no reason why the love of beauty should make anyone feel guilty. God himself is the supreme loveliness, summa pulchritudo (DQ 44). It is that which is beautiful which evokes our love. Augustine's God is not just the supreme Judge imposing moral duties and thinking enjoyment corrupt and wicked. Provided enjoyment is reserved for ends, not for things which are mere means, that is what God intends.

## Aesthetic Beauty

Augustine's conversion is a turning not from a hedonistic appre-
ciation of the beauty of the senses to a solemn morality of
joyless conscientiousness, but a turning from a lower good to
a higher one, from an inferior beauty to the supreme. Towards
this divine beauty his heart is 'inflamed with love'. Augustine
is aware that love (*amor*) often means a mere physical cupidity
(*libido*). Sometimes he recommends the use of 'affection' (*dilectio*),
the Latin word stressing the psychological, familial love without
erotic overtones. But he has no real reservations about the use
of *amor* to speak of human love for God. His repeated point is
that the object of our love, whether high or low, is the magnet
irresistibly drawing us on. We become what we love (*EP* 122. 1).
Naturally he concedes that what makes something beautiful is its
form and colour. The beauty of a human body is real beauty,
and in that there is no evil (*VR* 74). The loveliness and design of
the natural world are an expression of the underlying harmony
given by the Creator. Even 'evil' is the darkness which is only
the absence of light. Shadows have much to do with the beauty
of a landscape; dissonance enhances music. Human history itself
is a 'very beautiful song' in contrasting moods of glory and
tragedy; antitheses give greatness to a fine poem. God transcends
both colour and form. In him there is no shadow. Following
the Neoplatonists, Augustine speaks of form as imprinted on
matter by the divine giver. 'Form is what gives unity to anything.'
Therefore to contemplate beauty is to be pointed upwards to its
source. Even earthly beauty may help the upward look towards
the highest beauty in God.

Augustine knew about and much disagreed with puritan Christians who wanted to exclude music from worship. Words find their way to the heart and mind more effectively when sung than when said; for there is a hidden kinship between the soul and music (*C* 10. 33. 49–50). But let music's beauty point beyond itself. Augustine writes with a touch of irony of 'the many for whom happiness consists in the music of voices and strings, and who count themselves miserable when music is lacking to their lives' (*LA* 2. 13. 35).

# 8

# DIVIDED CHRISTIANS

A T Hippo the flock which Bishop Valerius entrusted to Augustine was, at least for his first ten or twelve years as bishop, only a small minority of the Christians in the city. The overwhelming majority in the province of Numidia were Donatists, adherents of the African schism led by Donatus in the aftermath of the great persecution of Diocletian. Most citizens of Hippo acknowledged as their father-in-God Proculeianus until about 407, then his successor Macrobius; not Augustine at all. The schism, established since 312, had become increasingly inveterate, invincible to either kindness or coercion. It originated in a protest against the 'softly softly' policy of the bishop of Carthage, Mensurius, and his archdeacon Caecilian. They discouraged zeal in opposing the edict requiring the surrender (*traditio*) of the sacred books and vessels. In 303 Mensurius had satisfied the friendly authorities by surrendering heretical volumes; another bishop handed over medical treatises. Casuistry went to ingenious lengths. When Mensurius died in 312, Caecilian was hurriedly consecrated to succeed him at Carthage, without waiting for the advent of the primate of Numidia, who claimed a customary right to preside for which there was no doubt some precedent. Zealots alleged that Caecilian's principal consecrator, Felix bishop of Aptugni, was among those guilty of surrendering Bibles and church plate nine years previously. The Numidian bishops came to Carthage in force and consecrated a rival to Caecilian. The dispute came to the attention of Constantine the Great, whose government officials were uncertain which bishop to deal with. Constantine referred it first to the see of Rome, then as a court of appeal to a council at Arles, both verdicts going against the Numidian opposition to Caecilian. By 313 this opposition was led by Donatus, who gave his name to the protest movement. Against the two ecclesiastical verdicts the Donatists appealed to the emperor himself. He declined to support them but 'left them to the judgement of God'.

The failure of the Donatists to win over the emperor dramatically helped to perpetuate among the Donatists an attitude of alienation from the government. The emperor had shown himself in their eyes to be in the arms of Satan and to belong to Babylon, not to Jerusalem. Donatus would therefore lead the Church of the Martyrs, a resistance movement against all compromise with those who thought it possible to suspend Christian worship at the command of an emperor. Cyprian, mid–third–century martyr, was also patron of the Donatists' sacramental theology—a doctrine of the Church as a gathered society, apart from the world and closed to its influence. Donatist laymen did not renounce their secular professions, but the group's doctrine of authority was focused upon their bishops, and accorded the minimum of acknowledgement to the secular power except insofar as property is held under the authority of the state.

The schism occupied a vast amount of Augustine's time and energy. His anti-Donatist writings are the largest single source of information we have. The nerve-centre of the Donatist position is a single axiom: the surrender to secular authority of the sacred books or vessels of the Church of God is an act of apostasy, no venial sin but a mortal strike against the holiness of the Church. To treat surrender on a par with, say, theft (i.e. as a highly reprehensible but nevertheless, for the Church, forgivable sin), is to misconceive the gravity of the act. An apostate brings a contagion passed to the innocent by the laying on of his polluted hands, bringing defilement like the offering of the eucharist by a priest in a corrupt Church. If therefore the churches in Italy, Gaul, Spain, or the Holy Land decide to be in communion with Caecilian and his successors at Carthage rather than with Donatus, this proves how insidious and catastrophic the contagion is. Except in Numidia the whole world lies in the devil's arms. The support given to Caecilian and bishops in communion with him by the imperial government merely provides additional evidence of Satanic activity. Truth is never found in a compromising, respectable establishment but always in a minority. Noah's Ark, containing only eight persons, is a type of the true Church.

Throughout North Africa two rival hierarchies were created. Most towns had two bishops presiding in separate basilicas over communities whose mutual estrangement the rival bishops had an interest in maintaining. The Donatists even sent a bishop to Rome to care for the African colony there. (Relations became tense when in 386 the man was expelled from Rome and, in Africa, began to give unacceptable orders apparently on Petrine authority to the Donatist bishop of Carthage Parmenian.) The Donatist heartland always lay in Numidia. They compensated for their failure to earn respect in other provinces by quoting the declaration of the bridegroom in the Song of Songs that he liked to 'rest in the south'. They also claimed Simon of Cyrene as a hero of African faith.

The Berber peasants of Numidia were tough, and did not cease to be so when they became Christians. In Numidia the conflicts between Christianity and paganism took aggressive forms. The rural Christians formed bands of men, vowed to celibacy and a homeless, nomadic life. They called themselves 'militants', *Agonistici*. Their primary role was to disrupt pagan festivals, smashing the flutes and pipes of the bands (*symphoniaci*), thereby intentionally provoking reaction from pagans in hope of a heroic martyrdom. Augustine says they did not actually smash idols, which would have been meritorious, but wished only to be killed themselves. The militants were devoted to the honour of their martyrs, erecting shrines to their memory, and gathering on their anniversaries to sing popular hymns in their praise and to drink at least as much wine as their pagan opponents consumed on feast-days. Most of them came from the high plateau of southern Numidia and spoke Punic. Numidian landlords wondered if they feared them as much as the arrival of the Roman legions sent in to keep order. The militants sided decisively with the Donatist cause, and became a private army. They were nicknamed by the Catholics 'Circumcellions', because they wandered about the martyrs' shrines (*circum cellas*). Their methods with pagan festivals brought odium on the Church. Augustine grants that their targets included some gross obscenities deserving to be stopped, but his own policy (fatally compromising in Donatist eyes) was to dismantle pagan shrines only when Christians owned the land; *cuius regio eius religio*.

About 345–7 the imperial government sent a commissioner named Macarius to Numidia to coerce the Donatists into submission. Donatus inquired 'What has the emperor to do with the Church?' Macarius' oppression was bitterly resented; he acquired a reputation as a hanging judge, and in retrospect the Donatists looked back on him in the way that Irish Catholics have thought about Cromwell or French Protestants about Louis XIV. In protest against Macarius the militants threw themselves over cliffs; some incinerated or drowned themselves. These suicides were passionately venerated as heroes as much as those who lost their lives disrupting pagan festivals. Stones inscribed with names have been found at the foot of precipices in southern Numidia. After Macarius each suicide was one more propaganda victory in a struggle against a satanic government in league with a polluted Church. The suicides fuelled hatred against a bewildered Catholic community which could not understand how it could be responsible if fanatics chose to take their own lives. Suicides especially recurred whenever government pressure was increased upon the Donatists. Leading Donatist bishops were embarrassed by the militants' self-destruction, but their people felt differently. Statements from Donatist bishops condemning the violence and suicides were usually muffled, since the Donatists throve on a sense of persecution, and felt that the government's inflexibility was to blame for the situation. Moreover, under Julian they had recovered confidence, as property confiscated by Macarius was restored to them.

Parmenian, the Donatist bishop of Carthage until 391, gave his party strong leadership. Without acknowledging the least responsibility for the violence and the suicides, he argued that the mere fact of Catholic persecution proves the Donatist community to be the true Church. No body can conceivably be the Church of the Crucified if it is willing to see devout men arrested and harassed by secular judges.

The 'times of Macarius' marked a turning-point in two major respects that profoundly affected the situation facing Augustine. First, the militant Circumcellions found a second target for their holy war, in addition to pagan festivals, in Catholics and their churches—with the additional attraction that the Catholics often did not defend themselves. Here, the Donatists felt, were the new prophets of Baal such as Elijah had slain at the brook Kishon. Armed with cudgels called 'Israels' and with a petrifying warcry *Deo Laudes* 'Praise to God' evidently intended to echo the last words of dying martyrs, they would ambush Catholic travellers, inflicting terrible injuries and loss of life. Sometimes a blinding mixture of lime and vinegar was thrown into the eyes of their victims. Large parts of Numidia became virtually a 'no-go' area to Catholic clergy. Augustine himself once escaped a full-scale ambush only because his guide took him by the wrong road in error. Augustine's biographer Possidius, bishop of Calama near Hippo, where Donatists were particularly strong, precariously survived a ferocious onslaught.

Sometimes the Circumcellions burnt Catholic churches; more usually they preferred to douche the floor with disinfectant, to show that they classified the basilicas with public lavatories, or would cover the walls in whitewash perhaps in censure of the growing Catholic custom of decorating walls with pictures of Christ and the apostles. They seldom left without smashing the altar. Intimidation was widespread. Catholic bishops were told that if they did not voluntarily keep silent, violent men would impose it on them. Circumcellion raids were often supported by equally dedicated young women, and usually masterminded by the Numidian country clergy.

Councils of Donatist bishops deplored the atrocities and proclaimed that no one can be justified in resorting to violence. When in 407 a new Donatist bishop was installed at Hippo, he was escorted into town by a massive Circumcellion force evidently intended to warn Augustine and his congregation. The new bishop, however, infuriated this embarrassing supporters' club by a sermon through a Punic interpreter, telling them to leave the city quietly without vandalizing Catholic property. (He would have to live there after they had gone home.)

Circumcellion muggings and arson were especially visited upon converts from Donatism to Catholicism. Conversions in either direction caused resentment. At Hippo Augustine had difficulty in persuading his congregation to be civil to Donatist fellow citizens when the rival community won back two deacons whom they had lost to Augustine for a time. For a Catholic landowner to reclaim at law land invaded by Donatist squatters or to take a Donatist debtor to court was to invite assault on oneself and one's family. If a Catholic landlord had Donatist serfs on his estates, he might find them instigated to rebellion. Such occasional acts of sedition were rare, and embarrassed the Donatist bishops who certainly did not understand their movement as a social or republican revolution. They used to promise molested landlords full restitution, but were subjected to some intimidation by their own extremists and must have hoped that somehow they would not have to implement their promises.

More than one modern historian has asked whether the Circumcellions were really social revolutionaries using religious dissent and alienation from the emperor to cover a secular cause. The militant Circumcellions may well antedate the rise of the schism, since their original target was paganism. The schism itself originated on a point of religious principle, as a split among the bishops made more bitter by personal animosities, and not as a social uprising. Donatism was, first, a religious struggle which came to make secondary use of social and perhaps economic factors. There was some 'Africa for the Africans' pride, and more than a touch of Punic local patriotism. One Donatist preacher claimed that Donatus himself is the 'prince of Tyre' of Ezekiel's prophecy (Ezekiel 38). Punic Christians were aware and proud of links between their culture and the Phoenicians of the Old Testament. But Augustine shows that Catholic Africans shared in such feelings as strongly as the Donatists. Even Augustine is gratified to discover the Old Latin version of Joshua 15 fixing the position of Jerusalem in relation to Africa. His predecessor Valerius learnt that the Punic *salus* means three, and suggested that the Punic Christians thereby disclose salvation (*salus* in Latin) in the Trinity. Augustine wished he could believe it true.

Good evidence shows the Donatists identifying the empire with the Babylon of the Apocalypse of St John. This work received a commentary from the liberal Donatist scholar Ticonius about 380 in which, we are told, he interpreted the book 'spiritually, not carnally', i.e. as no handbook for insurrection. Augustine never tires of pointing out how often Donatists themselves appealed to the emperor to get what they needed.

Circumcellion violence was sometimes restrained in the rural areas out of fear of the retribution Catholics in turn might exact (and evidently on occasion had exacted) in towns where Donatists were not so numerous. From this it is obvious that at least in some places the Catholic population was stronger in town than in countryside. Nevertheless the pattern emerging from the evidence is never a simple antithesis of opposing monoliths, i.e. we do not have an urbanized, Latin-speaking Catholic bourgeoisie in conflict with a rural Punic-speaking Donatist proletariat. In Numidia most of the towns were solidly Donatist, and the Catholic presence was precarious. It was common for the peasants on an estate to be of the same allegiance as their landlord; and in Numidia the peasants on Catholic land were often tenacious about their religious tradition in face of intimidation. If an estate was sold at auction, it might change from Catholic to Donatist hands (or vice versa), and awkwardness could then result. The Donatist bishop of Calama near Hippo bought at auction a nearby estate, and promptly rebaptized all the farm-workers under threats of violence, pleading that Catholic landlords had done the same in the past. Government coercion pressed many urban Donatists to change sides early in the fifth century, the rural areas to the south remaining intransigent, and this brought about a broad difference between town and country. But the town/country tension was more a consequence than an initial cause of the schism's history.

The second major consequence of Macarius' oppression was to harden Donatist rejection of Catholic sacraments. Donatus in 313 had stood by Cyprian's doctrine that Church and sacraments are inseparable. If, therefore, someone asks to be received who had been baptized by a heretic, schismatic, or an apostate (e.g. a *traditor*), his baptism is absolutely null and utterly void; indeed it is an actual injury which the authentic Donatist sacrament alone can heal. During the first half of the fourth century not all Donatists were strict in baptizing converts from the Catholic communion. After Macarius the line was rigorous, though gentle Donatist bishops would apologize for the apparent discourtesy inherent in their doctrine of the nature of the Church. The rebaptisms and reordinations caused intense anger to Catholic bishops, who felt the Donatists to be not merely insulting but also grossly ignorant of the truth that the sacraments belong to no man or human party but to Christ himself. The Donatists knew that if ever they admitted the validity of Catholic sacraments, they had lost their *raison d'être*.

Distress was caused if the son or daughter of a Catholic bishop married a Donatist. Mixed marriages between Donatist and Catholic were common in which neither partner would receive communion at the other's eucharist. Augustine himself had a Donatist cousin. Many Africans felt indifferent between the rival communions. Donatists rejected Catholic sacraments, while Catholics wholly accepted both baptism and orders in converts. So several people acted on the principle 'just in case': they went to the Donatists first for baptism, and then came over to the Catholic community. Paradoxically the offence given to Catholics by Donatist rejection of the validity of their sacraments was minor in comparison with the offence taken by Donatists when converts to Catholicism were accepted with a handshake or laying on of hands in token of recognition and restoration. But the Catholics declared one must be a member of the Catholic Church to be sure of salvation. One Donatist bishop outraged Augustine by replying to a proposal for joint public debate with words which acquiesced in the permanent and irremediable fact of schism: 'You keep off my sheep and I will keep off yours' (*EP* 21. 2. 31; *E* 105. 1). In Donatist eyes Catholic attempts at ecumenism were motivated largely by a desire to take over property, an ambition for the power and the glory. Large estates had been bequeathed to Donatist churches before the government declared such legacies invalid. Donatists also had a large stake in the money-lending business. They were far from poor. The group rivalry generated prejudice. Some Donatists believed that at mass the Catholic clergy placed something unmentionable on the altar; the notion that it might be holy communion seemed ridiculous to them (*E* 93. 5. 17). Anger, Augustine observed, passes into hatred if unhealed.

On Augustine's side the nerve-centre of the argument against Donatist is the proposition that a body confined to Africa cannot claim to be the worldwide Church which the prophets foretold and which the apostles of Christ set out to realize. As for their excommunication of the rest of Christendom the entire world judges unperturbed (*securus iudicat orbis terrarum*: *CEP* 3. 4. 24). The Donatists show how little sense they have of the universality of the Church by their own fissiparousness. Augustine points to the splits within the schism, above all in 392 when two competing factions for the succession to Parmenian at Carthage were reconciled only by the strong-arm methods of a colour-ful buccaneering bishop, Optatus of Thamugadi (Timgad, an outstanding archaeological site in southern Algeria, where the remains of Optatus' basilica may be seen). Optatus intimidated the opposition by mobilizing Circumcellion bands to the attack. He became a friend of the rebel Gildo count of Africa and fell with him in 398. His participation in sedition embarrassed many Donatists whose alienation from the government was ecclesias-tical rather than political. Donatism was weakened both by the internal schisms and by Optatus' support for an anti-imperial cause.

In his anti-Donatist argument Augustine happily exploits Optatus and other Donatist delinquents; but he had no illusions that the Catholic Church was or could be in this life a perfect society of saints. Noah's Ark, he remarks, included numerous malodorous beasts besides the eight rational souls, to whom the inconveniences of the voyage were endurable only because the tempest meant certain destruction to anyone getting off the boat. The parables of the kingdom (Matthew 13) portray the Church as a field in which wheat and tares grow together until harvest; the fisherman sorts out the good fish only when he has reached the shore. Scandals never offer sufficient reason for leaving the Church. That Church which St Paul declares to be 'without spot or blemish' is not on this earth.

To Augustine sacraments are God's works of power, to which the clergy are only ministerial and subordinate. God's grace does not depend for its action on the personal holiness of the minister or of the corporate body he serves. Augustine is appalled by a Donatist thesis he finds in Parmenian that the bishop is the very mediator between God and man. This, Augustine comments, confuses the apostolic principle that the only mediator between God and man is Christ himself, and uses language offensive to Christian ears, the very voice of Antichrist (*CEP* 2. 8. 15). Parmenian thinks the apostolic succession (a succession which Augustine himself did not think unimportant) a guarantee maintaining its value even in isolation from the universal communion it is intended to serve. For Augustine, therefore, sacraments duly given even outside the Catholic Church are valid but become effective means of grace only when the recipient is reconciled with the one Catholic Church. The learned Cyprian, to whom the Donatists confidently appeal, can indeed teach us much about the one Church, but about the sacraments the teachable Cyprian has something to learn (*B* 5. 26. 37). A valid sacrament, even in schism, can inflict no injury. But only in the blessed company of Catholic people is it an instrument of grace.

With profound feelings Augustine loves Mother Church, the very Dove of the Song of Songs or of Noah's Ark or of the Holy Spirit—*columba mea*, a source of infinite gentleness on which Augustine can become lyrical. This body with its head is the 'whole Christ' (*totus Christus*), called to exercise a priesthood which is that of the entire community, not merely of bishops and presbyters (*CD* 20. 10).

For Augustine the holiness of the Catholic Church is assured by its unity and uniqueness, not by being closed against the secular world. In his anti-Donatist writings 'the catholic communion' is synonymous with 'the communion of the emperor'. He in principle denies any transmission of pollution invalidating all ordinations originally associated with a bishop guilty of apostasy. 'Whether my great-grandfathers were or were not guilty of surrendering sacred things is a matter about which I care very little.' Between Donatist and Catholic there is no difference of dogma, Bible, or liturgical form. They used the same lectionary and psalm cycle. Yet the schism is irreconcilable: the Donatists are in schism first and foremost because they are in schism: and community rivalry is self-perpetuating. The two communities lived (and fed their children) on incompatible accounts of how the schism began. To invite Donatists to consider the past of their own group was often to be met by 'Do you expect me to sit in judgement on my father?' Augustine undertook a most careful documentary investigation of the history of the schism. He fast learnt how inferior oral evidence is to contemporary documents, and gathered a large dossier from public and ecclesiastical archives, both Catholic and Donatist. Donatist archivists were reluctant to give him access, but somehow he obtained what he needed, sometimes no doubt through converts.

Augustine was aware that large schemes of theoretical explanation can be shattered by a few very awkward facts. He had learnt that in his disillusion with the Manichees. He became the moving spirit in a series of Church councils at Carthage to give the Catholic bishops a united front. His indefatigable pen poured out polemical tracts in profusion; not, for the modern reader, enjoyable because they are repetitive and remorseless, but they are certainly masterful. For the people he composed an anti-Donatist acrostic hymn to instruct them in the origins of Donatism. The trochaic metre ignores all classical quantities and is based on stress. Each stanza is answered by a refrain, evidently sung to an easy chant: *Ómnes quí gaudétis de páce, Módo vérum iúdicáte.*

## Coercion

In 404 the Catholic bishop at the Donatist stronghold of Bagai, Maximinian, after regaining by court order a Catholic basilica seized by Donatists, was assaulted in his church. The altar was smashed over his head. His groin was slashed with a machete, and the fearful wound stanched only by the thick dust through which the attackers dragged his body. Momentarily his people recovered him, but then lost him again. The Donatists carried him off, finally throwing him off a tower where he landed in soft ash and was left for dead. A passing pauper later came to relieve himself at the place, and found the half-dead bishop. He called his wife, who had been modestly standing at a distance, and they transported the body back to the Catholics who, they knew, would reward them beyond the dreams of avarice. Maximinian was nursed back to health, and travelled to Ravenna there to show his ghastly scars to the emperor. Anger against the Donatists boiled over, and an edict was issued at long last classifying Donatism as a heresy, the profession of which brought civil disabilities.

For some years previously the Catholic bishops in Africa had been debating the wisdom of invoking the protection of the state. The edict of 405 was much stronger than Augustine thought wise at the time. Frankly insincere conversions took place among property owners, and Circumcellion terrorist raids were sharply increased. Augustine was at first opposed to coercion not on grounds of principle but for practical reasons. The emperor had a right and a duty to quell violence; and as a Christian prince he should also discourage error and disunity. But would not coercion produce feigned conversions and fill Catholic churches with sullen hypocrites? The Church (Augustine felt) already had enough hypocrites on its hands without welcoming people who made no secret of their lack of conviction. Gradually he was brought round to another view by the success of the policy. At Hippo about 390 the Donatist bishop could forbid the bakers to bake bread for Catholics. But now the city was largely converted to Catholicism. The military presence sent to enforce the edict removed fears from converts. Augustine was troubled by the conviction of fellow Catholics that religious freedom is a fundamental right and that it is in principle wrong for the state to offer more than reasoned persuasion. He sought a theoretical defence of the policy.

Every son is disciplined for his good by a conscientious father. It is absurd of the Donatists to treat a corrective flogging as worth an annual commemoration. Let there be no torture or capital punishment even of those responsible for murdering Catholics. The courts should impose fines, which will then be remitted on the intercession of Catholic bishops. But severity is not incompatible with love. In Christ's parable of the wedding feast the lord says 'Compel them to come in', *cogite intrare*. Fraternal love will not abandon all to eternal loss out of fear of what transitory pain now may do to a few (*E* 185. 3. 14). Because the hatred of the schismatics has become inveterate and because human pride and obstinacy are what they are, no reasoned persuasion gets through, and a shorter way is needed. Those initially converted by fear or self-interest learn in time to have inward conviction.

Augustine's conversion to the use of coercion brought sharp criticism from some fellow Catholics. In later ages his arguments came to be disastrously exploited by inquisitors, ecclesiastical and secular, who neglected his crucial proviso that the form of correction must be seen to be a loving familial chastisement, a minimal force, absolutely excluding torture or death even for cases of violence.

In 409, with a pagan proconsul installed at Carthage, coercion was suddenly replaced by toleration, and a number of ex-Donatists left the Catholic Church again. Augustine lost one of his own deacons at Hippo. Toleration, however, prefaced the possibility of talks. Augustine had long felt that public disputations enabled waverers to come over. A great colloquy at Carthage was planned for May 411, under the presidency of an imperial commissioner, the tribune Marcellinus, who was a Catholic friend of Augustine. Under order the Donatist bishops assembled in strength; and Carthage was full of several hundred bishops. Augustine was chief spokesman for the Catholics, Petilian of Constantine (an ex-Catholic lawyer) for the Donatists. The minutes of the colloquy transcribed in shorthand make compulsive but tragic reading. The Catholics began with a generous offer: if the verdict was in favour of the Donatists, the Catholic bishops would resign their sees and surrender everything to the Donatists. If the verdict was for the Catholics, then they would invite the Donatist bishops to share in collegiality with them without loss of dignity. If this coexistence was unacceptable to the congregations, both bishops would resign to make room for a third. Nevertheless collective rancour was too great. From the start the Donatists refused to sit down with the Catholics, so that everyone had to stand all day through the heat and dust. Marcellinus acted as arbitrator with exemplary fairness. At the end his verdict favoured the Catholics; but the Donatists thought it ludicrous to expect him to be impartial, and rejoiced to have won a famous victory. They took revenge on Marcellinus in 414 by delating him as party to a conspiracy against the emperor, for which he lost his life. But the main function of the colloquy was to justify the government in applying renewed pressure on those found to be in the wrong, imposing deprivation and exile on clergy and confiscating basilicas. Around Hippo resistance was strong. One Donatist bishop tersely declared that if the authorities came to take his basilica, he and his people would set fire to it with themselves inside.

In retrospect Augustine felt insincere conversions to be a less severe problem than he once feared. Some ex-Donatists manifested far greater personal devotion and virtue than Catholics of long standing. The quality of the Catholic bishops and congregations did not always impress the new adherents. At one little Punic-speaking town named Fussala 40 miles from Hippo, a new bishop put in by Augustine behaved with such folly that the ex-Donatists wondered what they had been forced to join, and Augustine felt so ashamed as to contemplate resignation (*E* 209).

In the deep south of Numidia intransigence was undiminished, and there the Donatists lingered on through both the Vandal conquest (430) and Justinian's reconquest a century later. The schism was finally submerged by the Arab invasion of the seventh century, and Circumcellion zeal was continued in the Moslem marabouts. But insofar as the Catholic cause triumphed, the principal architect of the victory was Augustine.

# 9

# DISCERNING THE TRINITY

WHEN before his conversion Augustine was reading the books of the Platonists at Milan in 385–8, he counted himself a catechumen—a term then implying no actual commitment to instruction for baptism, but at least occasional attendance at church services without sharing in the communion in the second half of the eucharist. His belief about Christ at this time was that he was an exceedingly wise man, the summit of human moral excellence; but what might be meant by 'the Word made flesh' passed his comprehension. An experiment in Plotinian mystical ecstasy was transient and left him feeling that 'it seemed like a memory of a delicious meal he had a chance to smell but not to eat' (*C* 7. 17. 23). But could there be a way if the very Word of God had come to our inferior world to raise us to himself and so make a reality of Platonic language about the soul's return to its origin in God? Only a mediator belonging equally to both realms, divine and human, can link the two. And that, Augustine discovers with astonishment, is just what the Church believes about Jesus Christ, the supreme example of grace.

Augustine could not make this belief fully his own merely on authority without an act of understanding. But the movement of his mind was not from a belief in the incarnate Lord through to a doctrine of the Trinity. The paradox in Augustine's intellectual development is that Neoplatonic texts had already given him a kind of doctrine of the Trinity, admittedly a Trinity of emanation, which he especially found in Porphyry, whom he quotes to this effect in the tenth book of the *City of God* (*CD* 10. 23); Porphyry, however, expressly rejects any notion of incarnation and therefore of Christianity. Augustine deduces that it cannot be solely through the incarnation that the concept of God as Trinity becomes revealed to man. We begin the pilgrimage of faith with the humanity of the Son of God. (The young Augustine likes the phrase 'the dominical man', *dominicus homo*, which theologians of repute had used, but at the end of his life he came to think it dangerous.) He is the moral exemplar. Through him we learn the way of purification by which we may rise from sense to mind, from temporal to eternal. So, writing *On True Religion* in 390, Augustine suggests that we grasp the Trinity by reason, the incarnation by faith. He is confronting the most puzzling and defiant feature of Christianity as a Platonist sees it, namely that the divine disclosure is not of an abstract and timeless truth but is discerned through a personal life within the flux of history.

Augustine's early essays after his conversion and baptism tentatively explore ways in which a Neoplatonic Trinity and the Christian belief in one God who is Father, Son, and Holy Spirit might be brought together. The Roman orator Marius Victorinus had preceded him along this road. But Augustine steps out in a new direction owing surprisingly little to his predecessor. Gradually he finds a language for stating a Christian understanding of God which keeps selected Platonic themes, but purges them of assumptions irreconcilable with Christian belief. He sheds his mind of the Neoplatonic Trinity of automatic self-emanation. At first he seeks evidence of the Trinity in the act of creating; but then, in the last book of the *Confessions*, he suggests that the right place to look is in the soul of man. There is a trinity of being, knowing, and willing which is nevertheless within a united personality (*C* 13. 11. 12), and perhaps this provides a mirror or analogy from which it may be possible to ascend to God.

Western theologians before Augustine had spoken of the divine Trinity as manifested in the successive self-disclosure of God in creation, redemption, and the Spirit's sanctification in the life of the Church. The Father sends the Son in the incarnation; then the Spirit at Pentecost. In his years as a presbyter Augustine can be found appropriating this way of speaking. At about the time he was finishing the *Confessions,* he first embarked on a lengthy and ambitious study designed to bring together the various traditions of talking about God as Trinity. The work was not completed for twenty years, being frequently pushed aside by the burdens of his duties at Hippo, the load which in the nineteenth book of the *City of God* he declares he would find intolerable were it not that he also made time for the quest of truth—time which his biographer Possidius remembered as being found far into the night. The book *On the Trinity* is partly addressed to a Christian readership, but partly also for unconvinced but sympathetic readers who find in Christian language about the Trinity an obstacle to the acceptance of the faith and are thereby deterred from being more than flying buttresses in relation to the Church. The tone of the book is serene, and even where disagreement is being recorded, there is hardly any polemical touch, except in his dismissal of the Arians, who were not at the time a problem in Africa. For most of Augustine's life, practising Arians in Africa were rare birds, occasional migrants from the Greek East, until the Vandal threat brought Gothic soldiers to Carthage. Being as Arian as their Vandal opponents, they needed a basilica and a bishop with whom, in the last year or two of his life, Augustine had some minor sparring. Some Donatists who tried to make alliance with these Goths against the Catholics were quickly stamped on by their own leaders. In *On the Trinity* Augustine's argument is directed not so hotly against the Arians as against orthodox theologians who have met Arianism with ineffective and insufficient arguments.

Arianism originated with the theses of Arius, a dockland presbyter of Alexandria about 320, who tried to make Christian faith more intelligible to educated contemporaries by denying that the Son of God is identical with the Father in his being. Arianism derived its strength mainly from its ability to invoke several Biblical texts; it was a strongly biblicist heresy, inclined to set aside the tradition of Christian worship in favour of a Neoplatonic logic giving a Trinity on three grades or levels of divinity. The orthodox writers of the Greek East especially the Cappadocian Fathers (Basil, his brother Gregory of Nyssa, his friend Gregory of Nazianzus) spoke of one identical being of Father, Son, and Spirit who are not three Gods but three distinct realizations of his one being. (Except by approximation, the Greek term hypostasis is almost untranslatable.) Augustine felt that, despite all their disavowals of tritheism, they were working with a social analogy which failed adequately to safeguard the divine unity. For instance, they spoke of the Holy Spirit as 'proceeding from the Father', a proposition evidently based on Scripture (John 15: 26). But if this text is taken to imply that the Son does not share with the Father in this, Augustine sees that as threatening the divine unity and offering a toehold to Arianism.

Both Hilary of Poitiers and Ambrose before him had spoken of the Spirit's coming forth as being an act of both the Father and the Son; the language preferred by Augustine had good western tradition behind it. Neither he nor his western contemporaries knew about the creed associated in the Greek churches with the council of Constantinople (381) which enshrined the formula 'the Spirit proceeds from the Father'. Bishops from the Latin West had not been present at that council, and its special status (as the second ecumenical council) was first understood in the West long after Augustine's time. Complaints from the Greek East against the West on the score of having added to the Creed the words 'and the Son' (*Filioque*) first appear in the middle of the seventh century when a heretical, anti-Roman faction in the East brought this charge against Pope Martin I.

Augustine also felt reserve about past western language for affirming difference within identity. The New Testament presupposes the distinction of Father, Son, and Spirit, yet is also uncompromisingly monotheist. It offers no technical terminology. The formula 'one substance in three persons' was coined by the first writer of Latin theology, Tertullian about 200 AD. The term *substantia*, translating the Greek *ousia*, is accepted Latin usage for inner immateriality beyond external appearances, beyond all 'accidents' such as shape or colour or other variable and mentally detachable qualities. Augustine accepts that God is one 'substance', as long as no one imagines goodness to be an accidental quality of divine being. Unlike in man, in God it is not one thing to be, another to be good. God's attributes are not other than himself.

In Augustine's form of Platonism, the everlasting abstractions—universals, numbers, properties, kings, etc.—are not so much

created by God as part of the divine mind. In God there are
no accidents. So, with some swallowing, Augustine digests the
notion that God is one 'substance'. But 'three persons' causes
much difficulty. It suggests three quasi-human centres of mind,
will, and feeling, which can hardly be what is meant. Church
usage, Augustine notices, shares in the general incapacity of
most of our everyday language to express meaning exactly. Here
his axiom that concrete language is inadequate for concep-
tual thought emerges prominently. The mind thinks in physical
images, even about matters it knows to be non-physical. A trian-
gle is a mental concept, not a shape drawn on paper, which is a
mere visual aid.

Augustine's thinking about God is unitive. He takes up the
theme of the image of God in man's soul, and looks for an ana-
logical ladder by which reason may climb to glimpse something
of the being of God. That God is Father, Son, and Spirit is known
by faith as the structure of Christian belief. But we may still seek
to understand by cross-questioning the highest element in man,
'personality' as we might say (the word is not Augustine's). If God
is love, we may start from the lover, the beloved, and the bond
of love itself, by which is meant the will wholly directed towards
the object of love. Augustine builds up an ascending succession
of triads: being, knowing, willing (which modifies a favourite
formula of Plotinus, 'being, living, thinking'); then mind, its self-
consciousness, and its power to direct its will and love towards
itself. But below the upper level of the mind lies a deeper
intuition, for which Augustine's word is *memoria*. Remembering
fascinated him as a psychological phenomenon: sometimes under
the will's control, sometimes not so at all (so that old sights
and smells suddenly bring the past flooding back into the mind,

welcome or unwelcome). It lies below the level of consciousness, with those things which the mind 'knows but does not know that it knows'. In short, Augustine discovers the subconscious.

Because the image of God in man is damaged, man needs grace to heal him. There is no proud ascent to God by the unaided reason. Therefore to know God and to love him is a gift of his grace, of which in time and space the incarnate Lord is mediator. Yet because the movement of Augustine's mind grasped the Trinity before the doctrine of the incarnation made sense to him, his Trinity is understood primarily as static, timeless being, rather than as God apprehended through Christ's redemptive work and through the experience of the Holy Spirit in the sacramental life of the Church. Augustine himself told Euodius that he contemplated his work on the Trinity with misgiving, 'burdensome to write and within the intellectual grasp of few' (*E* 169. 1. 1). He felt painfully conscious of its shortcomings. He felt it to be a characteristic of Christianity that the basic essentials of its gospel are plain to the simplest mind, yet that its ramifications are of such complexity that a lifetime is nothing like enough to master them, even for the most gifted intelligence (*E* 137. 1. 3). The greatest to which we can aspire is often no more than 'learned ignorance' (*C* 12. 5. 5). 'There are many things for which no reason can be given; but that does not mean that there is none' (*E* 120.1. 5).

# 10

# TWO CITIES

*The Conflict between Paganism and Christianity*

THE Latin word *paganus* means either a rustic person or, in military jargon, a civilian. From about AD 300 Christians are found using 'pagani' to describe non-Christians who had not by baptism become soldiers of Christ and so were non-combatants against evil. In Augustine's time Africa retained many tenacious adherents of 'paganismus'. After the emperor Theodosius' legislation in the 390s, temples were closed and pagan sacrifice even incurred the death penalty, as the equivalent of black magic and treasonable sorcery. At Carthage in 398 the temple of the mother-goddess Caelestis (Tanit) was shut. In Africa as in northern Italy and some other parts of the empire, reaction to the new policy was vehement. At one town a bronze statue of Hercules was destroyed by Catholic zealots, anxious perhaps not to leave all the action to Circumcellions. The pagan populace answered with a riot in which 60 Christians died. At Calama Catholic protests against a pagan festival led to the burning of their church, followed, however, by a general riot against all authority with looting in which Christian youths participated as much as any pagan. Augustine told his people to leave the demolition of pagan idols to bad men and Circumcellions unless given formal authority by the magistrates. They should not invade estates owned by pagan landlords and destroy the shrines. First they should rid people of the paganism in their hearts. 'Pray for them, do not be angry with them' (S 62. 11. 17). On the other hand, his Christians should never accept invitations to dinner parties held in pagan temples, even if hoping for the patronage of their noble host to obtain some promotion in their career. Augustine tried to wean his congregation from fortune-tellers, astrologers, and amulets, while granting that, if they must have an amulet, it should be a miniature copy of the gospels. (Examples of just such amulets have survived in Egypt from this period.) He once declares that there would be a riot if a Christian at Hippo were detected keeping the Sabbath; yet the churches are full of people who make decisions only after consulting astrological almanacs, who begin no new undertakings on unlucky days, and openly declare 'I never start a journey on the second day of the month' (G 35).

Augustine had some success in converting practising astrologers, who would come to burn their books publicly. He makes the illuminating comment that such converts often came later to seek holy orders (EP 61. 23).

Gradually pagan celebrations became clandestine. Adherence to the old ways was tenacious among two main classes—the rich aristocrats and the peasants. The conversion of a senator could have consequences for all who worked on his estates, since they would be encouraged to follow their lord: *cuius regio eius religio*. One rich lady of Augustine's acquaintance increased the Christian population by buying slaves and arranging for their instruction and baptism. One Catholic bishop in Numidia found his people bringing their children to baptism, but also arranging for pagan sacrifice to be offered for their health and happiness. Thoughtful pagans who did not wish to be Christians tended to adopt one of two positions, sometimes both. Several in Augustine's time argued that all religions are fundamentally saying the same thing under divergent forms and, as they have the great social utility of underpinning morality and public order, should be quietly maintained. Augustine met a priest of Cybele, the Anatolian mother goddess whose cult was widespread in the late empire, who claimed that his gentle self-castrating shepherd-god Attis was simply the Christian Good Shepherd under another mythological form. An alternative move was to amass objections to Christianity. For this purpose Porphyry had provided an arsenal of weaponry. Some of his objections were philosophical, based on Platonic assumptions, arguing that incarnation, or any other form of divine intervention, implies a change in God, and change is incompatible with perfection; or that incarnation requires a proximity between God and corporeality which is incompatible with the truth that the soul is purged by liberation from the body. Other objections were historical difficulties about the Biblical narratives. Porphyry especially gathered instances of contradiction. According to the Christians, God in the Old Testament requires sacrifice, in the New Testament not so, and the change of mind suggests vacillating inconsistency. Porphyry also made much of the conflicting genealogies of Jesus in Matthew and Luke. Stories like that of Jonah in the sea-monster were merely ridiculous. Augustine on the other hand could reply by pointing to a vast skeleton of a marine creature washed ashore near Carthage, inside which numerous Jonahs could have been comfortably accommodated. The change from Old Covenant to New is no more unreasonable than the differences in education at divergent stages of ability, or than the different seasons observed by farmers for the sowing of crops. As for the incarnation, it is fundamental for Augustine that it never implies any change in God, and to suppose the contrary is simply gross misunderstanding.

Porphyry offered some criticisms of the gospel stories, suggesting petulance in the cursing of the fig-tree or in the destruction of the Gadarene swine. But he (and almost all pagans known to Augustine) held Christ's teaching in deep admiration. Porphyry found support in an oracle of Apollo for the view that Christ was an exceptionally wise man mistakenly deified by his disciples who then told legendary stories of his virgin birth and resurrection, physical ascension, and the eclipse at the passion, which at full moon would be impossible. Porphyry also pressed some moral difficulties: can men really love their enemies? Is the exclusion of remarriage after divorce realistic? Is Christianity compatible with military service or with a magistracy charged to suppress criminals and requiring the taking of public oaths? May a Christian possess wealth and property, lend at interest (without which commercial enterprise could not be financed), or observe elegance and refinement in style of life and in dress (especially for women)?

Soon after 400 Augustine wrote his *Harmony of the Evangelists*, the first book of which surveys these pagan complaints. A particular important criticism to meet was that the adoption of Christianity by the emperors had failed to improve the felicity of the times. Sometimes Augustine dismisses this objection with a rough counter-attack: by 'felicity' people usually mean that they want an increase in the world's prosperity and pleasures— more bread and circuses, more free love, and no bills to pay afterwards: How happy we should be if all our follies could be enjoyed without remorse or anxiety! (*CD* 2. 20). But the question became urgent for many minds when on 24 August 410 Alaric and his Goths captured Rome. It was a stunning blow to the old Roman world. Even Jerome burst into incredulous tears when the news reached his monastery at Bethlehem. Had not Christian apologists (notably Origen in his *Contra Celsum*) claimed that if the empire became Christian, God would protect it against barbarians? If St Peter had replaced Romulus as patron of Rome, what was he doing in 410? Many Christians thought the end of the world (which some had fervently expected in the year 398, just 365 years after Christ's death) really was imminent (*E* 122. 2). Augustine thought very differently: a weary world may indeed be nearing its end, but each generation has always thought its own times uniquely awful. Man dies. What is a city but its human inhabitants? A city can die too. Talk about Rome as 'the eternal city' savours of blasphemy. Let those Christians who ask about providence tell us where Scripture promises peace and tranquillity in this life. Life is always an unceasing tempest to serious people who accept their responsibilities, a holiday only to those who contract out. As Christian pilgrims we have here no continuing city. Virgil's famous line that Rome's role is to spare the vanquished and to humble the proud must now give way to the truth taught by St James that 'God resists the proud.'

## *The* City of God

Much of Augustine's thinking about Church, State, and Society had been formed by his polemical stance during the Donatist controversy, a stance which cannot be described as one of alienation from the empire. The idea of the two cities, of Christ and Satan, first occurs about 400 in his reply to the Donatist

Parmenian's critique of his confrère Ticonius (*CEP* 2. 4. 9). Impetus to use this language may have been given by Ticonius for whom the two cities expressed the schismatics' belief in two separate societies everywhere coexisting. For Augustine they do not merely coexist, but are mixed. Ticonius said the Lord's body has a right and a left side. Augustine thinks this implies some facility in distinguishing and that he should have spoken of the Church as a 'mixed body' (*corpus permixtum*). In his treatise *On Baptism* of 401, he tries to break down the Donatist defences, asking them to concede that within the baptized community there are those who live unholy lives, and if so, there may also be holiness outside the walls. 'Just as many sheep wander without, so many wolves lurk treacherously within' (*B* 6. 1. 1). Naturally Augustine does not think membership of the visible Catholic community a matter of indifference for one's ultimate destiny; he regards it as one sign of the elect that at least when they depart this life, they will then be within the Catholic peace. The spiritual city is normally located in, but not conterminous with, the Church diffused throughout the world. The earthly Church is not without qualification identifiable with the kingdom of God of which it is, nevertheless, the anticipation and sign.

In 412–13, in the aftermath of the colloquy of 411, Augustine was brought into close contact with the Carthage circle of aristocratic and high culture. In this circle they were discussing not merely rhetorical and philosophical problems of the kind that Augustine handled with extreme facility, but also questions about the credibility of the incarnation. The cultured pagan Volusian could not see how Christianity could be other than destructive of Rome's imperial interests, productive in time of the decline and fall of the Roman empire. Rome had fallen to Alaric and his Goths on 24 August 410. Was Christianity responsible?

In 413 Augustine began a full-length apologia, the twenty-two books of the *City of God*, which amid many distractions occupied him until 427. The title of the book marks a conscious contrast with the *Republic* of either Plato or Cicero, indeed of both. The central theme is the contrast between the earthly and heavenly cities, prefigured in the Biblical Babylon and Jerusalem or in Cain and Abel. In this world they are mixed until the Last Judgment. Pagans say 'the old polytheism brought peace, Christianity has meant catastrophe'. The raping of Christian virgins by Alaric's soldiers does not look like divine protection. Augustine's reply is that the story of old pagan Rome was one of war and calamity. There was rape in Lucretia's time. Augustine admires the Roman historian Sallust's trenchant indictment of Roman society with its 'private affluence and public squalor', eaten up with the vainglory of imperialist pride. If, despite all this, pagan Rome had qualities of greatness which Augustine grants, why should the gods have the credit?

The encyclopaedic scholar Varro (116–27 BC) provided most of Augustine's matter on Roman religion. Varro's own view was that, although the myths are false, the so-called gods being merely deified men, nevertheless men who suppose themselves to be of divine descent tend to perform better for the advantage of the state. The feeling that something approximating to infallibility is expected can make acts and utterances wiser than would otherwise be the case. Varro's case rests on the sophisticated sceptical view that, although there is but one god, the social fabric depends on continuing polytheism. On Varro's basis, however, Augustine cannot see any valid connection between Rome's imperial greatness and the old gods. If we are to believe Rome has a place in the divine purpose, we must look elsewhere than to the pagan pantheon.

No earthly state is free from overthrow either from without or, more commonly, by corrosion from within. By whatever means they first attain power, rulers are faced with the need to act with justice in the interest of their own survival, which requires some acquiescence on the part of the governed. 'Take away justice and what are governments but large-scale brigandage?' (*remota iustitia quid sunt regna nisi magna latrocinia?*: *CD* 4. 4). In its lack of true justice Rome mirrored too faithfully the earthly city. But all human history is a sombre picture of ceaseless war. Some look on the story as dumb fate. They are right in thinking there is a chain of causation in the historical process: nothing happens without a cause, and by 'chance' we mean an event whose cause we do not know. There is no such being as a goddess Fortune, no Lady Luck. All is in God's hidden providence.

In Rome's history there are moments of high virtue and courage, especially in the earliest period, which Rome is right to admire. Then there was no luxury. Theatres, obscene shows in honour of the gods, and other media of corruption had not yet become established. (Here Augustine has an eye on the Italian refugees packing the Carthaginian theatres and amphitheatre.) Rome then had simple unaffected patriots of integrity like Fabius Maximus, Regulus, or Cincinnatus (*CD* 5. 18 gives a long catalogue). And from their affection for their earthly country, citizens of the heavenly country would do well to learn. But lust for imperial domination brought a decadence of which Juvenal and Sallust bear eloquent testimony. On contemplating Nero's reign, may we not say that people have the government they deserve?

Augustine concedes that Rome's early wars were just (*CD* 4. 15). Moreover, 'a wicked ruler with corrupt motives may enact a good law' whose unintended benefits are a sign of providence at work (*LA* 1. 5. 12). But large empires easily lose sight of personal values in search of glory. Mankind is more happily governed in small units. With extraordinary prescience Augustine virtually writes a blueprint for the political organization of the barbarian kingdoms that will succeed to the western empire in the two generations after his death. But it is no warm hope of things to come. Alaric's invasion means only that 'the empire is afflicted, not changed into something different. It may well recover: who knows God's will?' (*CD* 4. 7). 'Rome will not perish unless the Romans do so; and they will not perish if they praise God. What is Rome if not the Romans who live there? It is no matter of stones and wood, of cloud-capped towers and gorgeous palaces' (*S* 81. 9 with a reminiscence of Plotinus I 4. 7. 23 which, Possidius reports (28. 11), was on Augustine's lips as he lay dying during the Vandal siege of Hippo in 430).

Nevertheless, among his contemporaries Augustine stands out by asking the question where things are leading to. Something deep inside him tells him that Rome, 'now growing old and waning as an earthly kingdom', is to fall like Babylon (*EP* 26. 2. 18).

Moreover, Augustine is opposed to exegetes who think Gog and Magog, whose armies 'march to surround the beloved city' (Rev. 20: 9), mean the Goths. There are Goths for whom God intends as much access to the kingdom as for the Romans. Christ's promise is to all nations, not to Romans alone (*E* 199.12. 47). Convert the barbarians to the faith and peace will follow or at least be much easier to negotiate (*E* 189. 5. 199. 12. 46). We live now in the 'Christian age' (*aetas Christiana*), in

'Christian times' (*Christiana tempora*). Rome's princes are now obedient to the one God. Their happiness lies in just government rather than in imperial conquests. Providence may grant believing emperors health, wealth, and long to live, as in the case of Constantine. Or it may not, as with Jovian and Gratian, cut off in their prime. Long life is no ultimate measure. Moral and personal values matter far more than military grandeur. Quality not quantity.

From the sixth book to the twelfth Augustine turns to the philosophers, especially to Plato and his modern expositors Plotinus and Porphyry. To the historian of ideas Augustine's critical review of Platonism is among the most remarkable sections of the work. Platonism was in his time the only system with living power; and 'no philosophers are nearer to us Christians than the Platonists' (*CD* 8. 5). But Augustine's thesis is in a nutshell, How near and yet how far! The Platonists are right that God cannot be a material body; he is unchangeable perfection and 'simplicity' (i.e. not compounded of diverse elements, but is what he is and has). Eternity and immutability are the same. But if the soul is changeable, the Platonists mistakenly regard that as a consequence of its presence in the body, rather than a result of its inherent instability as a created being. They rightly see that God is the sunlight of the soul, which cannot find happiness except by participation in God's light, and therefore needs purification to find its way to the immutable Good. They speak of the fall resulting from neglect and of the wings the soul needs to fly up home again. They explain evil as a consequence of free choice, as a subordinate presence setting off the good as shadows contrast with darkness, as non-being in contrast with the eternal Being which is God. Augustine has no hesitations in welcoming the Platonic/Aristotelian notion of a hierarchy or continuum gradually diminishing in being and goodness. (He accepts a thesis advocated by Porphyry that in fundamentals Plato and Aristotle are in agreement, thereby making room for Aristotle's logic within a Neoplatonic metaphysic.) Platonists are also right to affirm providence in the beauty of the created world, in animals and plants, and in the stars above; that the unjust ultimately harm themselves more than their victims; that not to receive corrective discipline is in itself a penalty. As Augustine contemplates the Neoplatonic vision of nature, man and God, it seems natural and fitting to him that in his time many of the students of Plotinus, 'after a few changes', have adopted Christianity.

But there are other Neoplatonists who have become intransigently pagan, who have taken up magic, and have developed an elaborate theology of pagan sacrifice to defend polytheism. (Augustine's reference is to Iamblichus and his Syrian school of Constantine's time.) In the latter case Platonism is being set up as a religious rival to exclude Christianity, at least for the intelligentsia. Augustine remarks that Platonism has not tried to become a popular philosophy in the way that Stoicism or Epicureanism did, and in the sense that Christianity is.

Late in the third century Porphyry himself anticipates this divide between the two wings of the Platonic school. He himself rejects the move towards involvement in cult, which he felt to be materialist and quasi-magical. He wished for a spiritual religion of mystical aspiration. Augustine's relationship to Porphyry is one of both pupil and adversary. In this respect he sees Porphyry as being at odds with himself, making vast concessions of principle to the Christians and yet hating them the more, the closer he approximates to their position and they to his.

The 'few changes' Augustine wishes to bring to Platonism are not as modest as the serene apologetic of the *City of God* would have the reader think. Plato, he thinks, had a theology incompatible with polytheism, yet compromised with it. Augustine accepts that the soul is immortal, not that it is coeternal with God himself and of the same substance as its Creator. Platonists speak of a divine world-soul. There is certainly a life-force (*vitalis virtus*) immanent within the world, but Christians think this is the gift of his creative energy, not God himself. They are agnostic whether or not there is a world-soul; only they are sure this world is not a god. The Platonic critics so divorce soul from body that they can make nothing of Christian language about resurrection. Yet the Platonists themselves, in defiance of the natural sense of the *Timaeus*, affirm the eternity of the material cosmos. They believe, with Plato, in the miserable doctrine of reincarnation, and simultaneously teach with Porphyry that 'we have to escape from everything corporeal'. They think nothing innovative or creative can occur in a cosmos which simply rolls cyclically on its everlasting way. Yet they talk of the soul being delivered from the treadmill; and if that is not a new departure, what is? (*CD* 12. 20). Augustine looks over his shoulder here at the doctrine of world-cycles which Origen had thought an unavoidable possibility if freedom is an eternal possession of all rational beings. Augustine felt that in Origen both heaven and hell are replaced by a vast purgatory in which all souls eternally rise and fall, leaving us in 'endless real misery punctuated by short periods of delusory happiness'. Above all, the Platonists cannot tolerate the incarnation because it is to them inconceivable that the very grandeur of God may be discerned in a supreme act of grace. Demosthenes once replied to someone asking him the three first principles of oratory that they are first, Delivery, second, Delivery, and third, Delivery. The Christians say the same of Humility (*E* 118. 3. 22). The incarnation is rejected where it is offensive to that pride to which it is God's answer. That is why in pagan Platonism, there can be no indispensable mediator, 'no tears of confession, no eucharist' (*C* 7. 21. 27).

The relation of time to eternity is central both in Augustine's theology and in his debate with Platonism. He is impatient both with Christians and with critics of Christianity who think eternal means everlasting in time, as if the eternal God is old and will eventually be very old indeed. Pagan critics mockingly inquire what God was doing before he made heaven and earth. Augustine is offended by Christians who make the ironical but cheap reply, 'making hell hotter for curious questioners' (*C* 11. 12. 14). Both question and answer presuppose misguided formulations. Plato saw rightly that eternity is not an infinite extension of time, but that 'time is a moving image of eternity'. But the Platonic school, strong on the immutability of God and the realm of Ideas, is weak on the changing historical process of the temporal order, 'which carries the human race as if down a river' (*T* 4. 16. 21). The Platonists are right to speak of God as transcending time, so that eternity is not the experience of successiveness and transience that man has, longing to hold on to some fleeting joy, fearful of the future, nostalgically thinking back on the past in the misery of recalling an irretrievably lost happiness. Man is split between his future and his past. It is his mortal condition to perish to make way for the next generation (*CD* 12. 4). God is eternal Now. Of course, Augustine is aware that here there are severe problems. It is not easy to define eternity in contrast with time until one has come to a definition of time,

And the definition of time is bafflingly difficult. 'I know what time is as long as nobody asks me' (*C* 11. 14. 17). Augustine reaches out towards the approach which will be adopted by Boethius in the *Consolation of Philosophy*.

Having weighed in the balance both the history of Roman government and the highest aspirations of Greek philosophy, from the eleventh book of the *City of God* onwards Augustine begins the description of the two cities. He seeks to offer a conscious alternative to Platonism, which can find little significance in the space–time process, and to discern a grand parabola of divine providence in human history. He traces the steps from creation to Satan's fall in pride and envy; the fall of Adam and the consequential disorder of man's affections; the divine remedy through the calling of an elect people, through the Hebrew prophets whose expectation culminates in the gospel; the coming of the one mediator Jesus Christ, and his pilgrim Church marching to the heavenly Jerusalem, the kingdom of God, which is already being realized in its proclamation and sacramental life. Against this Church the 'earthly city', through the agency of the Roman empire, launched the persecutions (schematized by some to correspond to the ten plagues of the Exodus, a view Augustine does not share).

Persecutions had discouraged the Early Christians from looking to the state for any moral benefit other than the suppression of wickedness. It was not natural to them to adopt the classical Greek estimate of the city-state as a positive good educating its citizens in virtue and, by justice, giving them greater opportunities for enjoying this life. To Augustine neither the Roman empire nor any likely form of government in this world resembled a realization of this ideal. He does not see the state as able to make men inwardly virtuous, but only as capable of restraining overt criminal acts. And yet man, so anti-social by corruption, is essentially social by nature (*CD* 12. 28). His selfishness leads to wars and conflicts far more ferocious than the wildest of beasts ever have (*CD* 12. 23). But he nevertheless has no greater longing in his heart than for peace.

Even in an unjust war, an individual soldier obeying orders is morally innocent (*F* 22. 75; *CD* 1. 26). Even just war is misery (*CD* 19. 7). But John Baptist did not require soldiers to leave the army (*EP* 118. 31. 1; *F* 22. 74; *E* 189. 4 to Boniface). The evil of war lies not in death but in cruelty, lust for domination. But for self-defence or to recover one's property force can be justified. To get the peace all love to achieve, strive for justice.

In this world the four cardinal virtues of justice, courage, prudence, and self-control are expressions of love, but, because they presuppose conflict, they belong to this world (as Cicero's *Hortensius* taught). Man's longing is for an ordered society of fellowship and love. This is something the state cannot create or maintain. Man accepts the authority of positive law because order is preferable to anarchy and chaos; but in laws man seeks some vestiges of a higher justice. Augustine does not think that even a wicked ruler making bad laws exercises a false authority that one is morally entitled to disobey. The threat of anarchy is too constant. But he hopes for a Christian emperor who will rule justly; will remember he is but man as he receives the flattery of his courtiers and subjects; will use his power not only to suppress evil but to foster divine truth; will be reluctant to punish, and where punishment is necessary will never act from personal animosity but seek to make it possible for the offender to amend; will eschew luxury in personal life, and realize that it is harder to master one's own passions than to rule over the greatest empire (*CD* 5. 24). Yet whether the emperor is Christian or anti-Christian, he has the right to be obeyed in all temporal affairs; it is in respect of our souls that we are to be answerable exclusively to God.

The emperor is in fact now a Christian. Does this mean that a pagan state has been replaced by a Christian state in which we may look for the kingdom of God? 'The emperor has become a Christian—the devil has not' (*EP* 93. 19).

The concept of a 'Christian state' is embryonic. Once (*GC* 2. 17. 18) he speaks of 'Christianum imperium'; he hopes the just laws of a believing emperor will regenerate society, tired of living sick at heart, scared of dying and make possible 'a just empire' (*E* 138. 2. 14).

Just as Israel has played its part in providence's purposes, so too a Rome obedient to Christ may do the same. If we ask what that consists in, the answer is in terms of the personal obedience of its citizens to the calling of God. So the fact that the emperor is Christian does not alter the essential character of the state as a mirror of the earthly city.

The identification of Babylon with the emperor's government and of Jerusalem with the Church sounds a lot more Donatist than Augustinian. His anti-Donatist writings generally adopt a positive view of the function of the state, especially invoking St Paul in Romans 13 (e.g. *E* 87. 7). But in the nineteenth book of the *City of God* he comes astonishingly close to a Donatist dualism of Church and State. They enjoy so little common ground that it is hard to see what the bishop of Hippo could say if the proconsul of Africa were to ask him what changes he would like to see in the organization and administration of government to make it more open to protecting those personal values he so rightly cares about. Augustine's political attitudes have received diametrically opposed interpretations, some seeing in him a dedicated patriot of the imperial idea, others the cold detachment of a monk who has renounced the world and will feel morally compromised if he now reverts to caring about its prosperity and welfare. Since both interpretations can cite texts of Augustine in their support, it is worth looking about for any alleviation of the contradiction. The paradox of Augustine is that he expresses himself in profoundly conservative terms about the existing Roman order precisely because he has himself renounced secular ambition and never sees the Church as having a secular role to perform which will not threaten to obscure its true purpose. He loved the poor and lived as one of them. He never thought he could conceivably be of service to them by leading them out in revolution. As for his estimate of the honours attaching to high office under the crown, he freely quotes the exhausted disillusion of the book of Ecclesiastes.

Augustine begins the nineteenth book of the *City of God* by laying down the lines of divergence. The philosophers of the secular world place the supreme good in this life—in pleasure, tranquillity, good health of body and mind, on top of which the individual will superimpose a life of reasonable virtue. Christians believe the supreme Good is in the city which is God's, transcending this order altogether. This life is ever beset by ineradicable sources of unhappiness, rooted in all we most value. What tensions marriage and family life may generate! The best of friendships can suddenly be shattered by death or by an utterly unpredictable and painful act of disloyalty. Friendship is the supreme solace in a life of misunderstanding and calamity. The closer your friend, the more pain his death brings. Augustine's lifelong agony was the fear of losing friends, and the passage seems to have the tribune Marcellinus in mind, perhaps others also.

A Christian offered appointment as a judge should without question accept. But in the courts the judge will at times find it hard to know if the defendant is innocent or guilty. The use of judicial torture universal under the empire is a practice to which here, in principle, Augustine offers no explicit objection (elsewhere he is wholly negative about torture). Here his objection is that in practice it can make it less likely the truth will be discovered, since torture makes innocent men confess to crimes they have not committed; and even if the torture ends by proving innocence, the wretched victim may well be maimed for life, if he does not die of his injuries.

All rulers in Church or State should forgo what Sallust calls 'the lust for domination', and should see their part as a service to those they govern. Roman society is in practice pervaded by the dominance of man over man, institutionalized in slavery. Like private property, slavery is not at all an ideal arrangement, and is a consequence of Adam's fall. But it is more than a simple consequence. It is, Augustine suggests, a divinely imposed penalty through which good order in society is also preserved. Slaves in good houses were better fed, housed, and clothed than day-wage labourers. Augustine's strong doctrine of original sin makes him profoundly conservative towards social institutions and structures, changes in which can only tinker with the problem. Moreover, a good father of a family has a duty to correct his children and his slaves by words and blows. Christianity, therefore, proposes no programme for the overthrow of slavery as an institution, and allows masters to have unsatisfactory slaves flogged or even chained if it be for their good. Its political programme is not one of levelling, because its programme is not political at all. Like Thomas Hobbes, Augustine sees man as so consumed by pride and cupidity that he can be held in restraint only by drastic systems of social control.

Again, Christianity does not deny that there is true virtue in the service given to society by a good man who is not a Christian. It says only that if this goodness is not acknowledged to be God's gift, his splendid service is flawed and ministers to pride. The pilgrim Church on earth, reflecting the heavenly city and journeying towards it, depends for peace on the earthly city: 'As long as the two cities are intermingled, we also enjoy the peace of Babylon.' But the heavenly city requires no change in laws, institutions, and social customs, except where they hinder the Church in the true worship of God. This does not mean that the citizens of the heavenly city, whose end is to contemplate God, have either a duty or a right to opt out of active participation in the business of daily life. Even holy leisure would become selfish if the call to active life, e.g. in the episcopate, were refused. Does not St Paul tell Christians to pray for kings and all in authority? Did not Jeremiah exhort the exiled Hebrews to pray for Babylonia, their place of captivity? Provided that they are not required to worship false gods, Christians loyally uphold order and government.

The *City of God*, then, is intended to allay the fears of educated pagans like Volusian, and to help them to recognize that in rejecting the falsity of polytheism Christianity does not necessarily spell the end of the empire or undermine its conscientious administration. Augustine is out to reassure, anxious to limit the Church's common ground with the secular world so as to leave the institutions of society as free of clerical intervention as possible. The overlap is a deeply shared interest in peace, whether in defence against the barbarians on the frontier or against threats of civil war. Otherwise let the secular world happily get on with its work without interference from the Church. Augustine exemplifies the way in which the Early Christians, especially the ascetics, create 'secularity', taking religion out of the everyday world of commerce, soldiering, litigation, criminal justice, and political decision. This world's rulers are necessarily concerned with solving short-term problems which can change dramatically in a week. The Church thinks in centuries. Its task is to be a vehicle of the proclamation of God's kingdom to the end of time. The world will be a happier place if public offices are held by humble and honest men of faith and integrity serving peace and justice. Although holders of high office can succeed only by being feared or loved (C 10. 36. 59), Augustine allows that there is no necessary link between power and pride. Once he expresses deep displeasure to a senior official at Carthage who was a catechumen and proposed to defer offering himself for baptism until after laying down his dangerous office. To be a good public servant is a religious as well as a civic duty.

Public appointments and the administration of justice in the Roman empire were badly afflicted by bribery and corruption which were endemic. Notoriously, next to nothing could be achieved at the imperial court unless suitable *douceurs* were put in the hands of the people who counted, and the palms of their various minions also had to be greased. Officials, having obtained their posts by expenditure that often involved expensive borrowings from money-lenders, thought it self-evident that they had a moral right to recover their costs, with a bit extra for the day when they lost their job because their patron had lost his. In the sixth book of the *Confessions* Augustine praises the exceptional integrity of Alypius at Milan when he was legal assessor to the finance officer for Italy. Alypius (not at that stage a Christian) withstood not only bribery but threats when a rich senator was attempting tax evasion. His integrity astonished his colleagues at the department. Similarly Alypius would never have books copied for his personal use at the special cheap rate to which government officials were entitled for necessary business, though the abuse was evidently almost universal. Augustine knew, as every thoughtful observer of the operations of government knew, that corruption bred not only injustice but inefficiency. He wanted men of religious principle and honesty to serve the administration and the lawcourts, and no small part of his sadness at the execution of his friend Marcellinus was due to his awareness that this was a good man of proved integrity with qualities possessed by too few.

Augustine never says or implies, and it is monstrous that he was (much later) taken to say and imply, that because secular power is by definition satanic, the summit of authority ought to be entrusted to eminent clergymen who can be relied upon to be altruistic. His writings frequently reflect his apprehensions when faced by worldly headline-seeking clerics among the African bishops, at whom his warning finger is shaken much more often than at powerful officials or landlords (though oppressive acts on their part would also bring a protest from Hippo of the type that Augustine supremely exemplified, combining candid rebuke with deep disappointment that an otherwise good person should be responsible for maladministration). Among his letters of remonstrance, none perhaps is more blistering than one to a rich man who had got himself elected to a bishopric as a device for concealing a vast tax fiddle (*E* 85).

If the piety and honesty of the individual members of society lie at the heart of a solution to society's problems, it is true at the same time that there is such a thing as the moral society. Augustine does not require goodness only of the individual. The quality of a society, he says, can be seen by asking what it loves: what, so to speak, it collectively spends its money on (*CD* 19. 24). If it devotes its resources to material comforts, it will end up as a mean affair. If it cares about higher things, culture, education, and religion, then that marks it out as a society of superior power. The price-tag that society places on things and on people reflects a moral decision. Augustine thinks it unedifying that a mentally deficient fool can be bought as a slave for a rich man's entertainment (*PM* 1. 22. 32 records pleasure at one such court fool whose intolerance of blasphemy among persons of high rank did much good).

The *City of God* is also an important attempt to establish a vantage-point from which a panoramic view of the history of the world becomes possible. It is not the last history of the world in short compass to leave its readers irritated by its superficiality. Augustine's concern with history, however, is exclusively theological. He is emphatic that the human race is a unity, a *massa*, whose history, in all its manifold diversity, may nevertheless be seen as a single story, sacred and profane intermingled.

# II

# FREEDOM AND GRACE

THE Italian refugees who moved to Africa to escape Alaric's Goths in 410 included a British monk who had acquired a considerable reputation in Rome, the layman Pelagius, earliest of surviving British writers. Disappointed not to meet Augustine, then absorbed in the Donatist colloquy of 411 at Carthage, he went on his way to the Holy Land. The two men saw each other in the distance but never talked; it is a symbolic non-encounter. Pelagius had received a good liberal education perhaps in Gaul, and, after travels in the East, had settled in Rome about 398 practising the ascetic life. In the capital he became a favoured spiritual director for some aristocratic families recently converted to Christianity and needing advice on the ordering of their lives and households. Pelagius was shocked by the moral compromises prevalent at Rome. The higher clergy had persuaded the upper-class families to begin to associate themselves with the Church. In many cases the allegiance was not yet deep, and scarcely altered their private lives. Pelagius saw hard sayings in the gospel about wealth, and warnings elsewhere in the New Testament about the uselessness of faith without works of love. If the calling of God is strenuous and sacrificial, costing rath more than a few charitable donations, Pelagius felt bound to the Roman Christians to take their duties more seriously. H also apprehensive at the success of the Manichee infiltration of the Catholic community in Rome, and at their appeals to the letters of St Paul. Pelagius therefore wrote a commentary on St Paul to make clear the need for dedicated ethical action. He sees, with some reason, that an ultimate dualism of good and evil may easily be conducive to moral lethargy. In the remission of sins in baptism, he teaches, there is a mysterious uncaused gift of God by grace alone by faith alone. No other writer of Christian antiquity speaks so incisively of 'faith alone'. But the path of holiness to be trodden by the baptized involves the most serious obedience to Christ's ethical commands. In his opposition to Manichaeism at Rome Pelagius found comfort in Augustine's three books *On Freedom of Choice* completed in 394–5; they were congenial reading to him.

At Rome the *Confessions* of Augustine quickly found their way in the bookshops. One day a bishop quoted in Pelagius' hearing the words 'You command continence; grant what you command, and command what you please.' To Pelagius it sounded destructive of moral responsibility. The tepid state of moral effort in the city was not surprising if Christians were absorbing this kind of doctrine. He was moved to protest. His commentary on St Paul and a succession of ensuing tracts explained that to sin is to make a choice for which we are responsible. It is not to be born with a taint inherited from Adam which is simply one's destiny. Naturally Pelagius recognizes the social pressure of the environment of bad example, into which each individual is born. He acknowledges the weakening of the will by decisions rough which the character is moulded. But all evil is in the never in the nature with which we come into the world hich is the Creator's glorious gift. In the Bible God gives commandments to help us, and a will to enable us to carry them out. God's help is not limited to an external list of rules. He puts pressure on our wills, excites us towards the good, and illuminates us to know the right path. But in the ultimate citadel the free will is unassisted in its decision to accept help. Grace may indeed initiate, but if so the will brings the act to completion.

Pelagius begins from responsibility as the foundation of moral action. He goes on to affirm the innocence of the newborn infant. If Adam passed on no sin, neither could he transmit any penalty for it. Adam needed food in the garden of Eden; so death must be natural rather than a divine punishment for sin. In the Greek East such teaching could have caused no special surprise, but in Africa it was to be different. In 411 Pelagius left behind at Carthage a lawyer named Caelestius who trenchantly developed his master's views. He applied for admission to ordination but was refused. He was reproached for teaching that Adam would have died whether or not he had sinned; that his sin was not transmitted to posterity; that both the law and the gospel are valid ways to heaven; that Old Testament saints lived sinless lives; that newborn infants are like Adam before the fall. Caelestius' reply was to urge that the question of original sin was intricate and open for discussion, not a formally defined dogma. When asked what sins are remitted in infant baptism, he laconically replied that he upheld the practice. He then departed for Ephesus to be admitted to orders there. But he left behind some at Carthage who were impressed. Soon news reached Augustine of some who taught that infant baptism confers a positive sanctification by the Holy Spirit but no negative remission of sins, the recipients being innocent.

Gradually Augustine became drawn into a slow crescendo of debate. At first he moved cautiously. Pelagius had powerful supporters at Rome whom it would be unwise to alienate. He was also a friend of Paulinus of Nola. In 413 Pelagius and Augustine actually exchanged brief letters cast in terms of formal courtesy. But soon the storm-clouds gathered. In 415 Augustine sent on to the Holy Land a Spanish presbyter named Orosius, a refugee from the barbarian invasions who had come to ask Augustine's help in answering the continued propagation of Priscillian's views in the Iberian peninsula. Orosius was sent to make contact with Jerome, and briefed to see that Pelagius won no following at Jerusalem. Jerome had a natural impulse to sharp controversy, and uttered warnings against Pelagius among the westerners in the Holy land. But Orosius and Jerome bungled the affair badly. A synod called to look into Jerome's charges was easily assured that Pelagius never supposed man could be saved without God's help. Pelagius was canonically acquitted of heresy. This conciliar acquittal caused consternation when the news reached North Africa. Augustine at once inspired two counter-synods to censure what must be called a malicious parody of Pelagian doctrine, and also elicited a negative judgment from Pope Innocent I. Fortified by two synods and a Roman verdict Augustine announced that, at least as a legal process, the Pelagian cause was finished: *causa finita est* (S 131. 10).

The matter turned out to be anything but finished. Three months later a new Pope, Zosimus, was scarifying the Africans by listening attentively to Caelestius' personal assurances of his complete orthodoxy and of his devoted wish to follow the ʾime authority of the apostolic see. Zosimus wished the ns respected Roman authority as much as Pelagius and his friends, and for a time it seemed as if he might reverse Innocent's unfavourable judgment. Alypius promptly sailed to Ravenna to influence the court. On 30 April 418 an edict abruptly expelled the Pelagians from Rome as a threat to peace. The emperor had been moved to decide over the heads of the hesitant pope, who now had no choice but to submit. Soon he died.

The Pelagian cause was then vigorously taken up in the West by its most brilliant advocate, Julian bishop of Eclanum near Benevento, son of a cultivated bishop with whom Augustine had once enjoyed amicable correspondence. Julian's controversial abilities were formidable in both eloquence and dialectic. It was the only time in Augustine's life when his antagonist had ability not far short of his own. Julian's reaction to Augustine is comparable to that of Erasmus confronted by Luther. A bonny fighter who had no compunction about delivering a few blows below the belt, he was also a superb writer of Latin. Even Augustine was constrained to concede that his Pelagian critics had 'great and sharp minds' (*E* 186. 5. 13). But it was painful when Julian exploited the *Confessions* as a source of injury to the old man now in his early seventies, and complained of his 'Punic logic', gossiping away to his Maker about his wine-bibbing mother and trivialities like the adolescent theft of pears.

The Pelagians were not a tightly knit school of theology, but a loose group of broadly like-minded ascetics or bishops who feared moral erosion if Christians came to think that every gift is so of grace, including the will, that they can simply sit back and wait for it to arrive. Between Pelagius and Julian differences can be found in detail, and in Julian the position is far more developed and sophisticated.

Among the factors which in 415 fanned smoking embers into flame was a book by Pelagius himself *On Nature*, in which his defence of freedom is supported by grateful quotations from Augustine's early anti-Manichee writings, especially that *On Free Choice*. The implication was understood: what a pity that the dregs of Manichaeism have remained to reassert themselves in this man who was once a sound libertarian.

The Manichees thought the evils of this world too massive to be explicable by the free-will defence. They saw evil in conflicts of interest. They thought Neoplatonic talk about evil as non-being would quickly change if you put a scorpion into the philosopher's hand (an argument which Augustine thinks unfair to the interests of the scorpion, which has its due place in the beauty of a diverse world). They also regarded sexual desire, especially because of its recalcitrance to rational control, as a principal means for the perpetuation of evil.

Although the Pelagian controversy meant a battle on the opposite front from Manichaeism, Augustine never moves from the view of evil adopted in his early writings. He continues to see evil as a consequence of a freely chosen, uncaused neglect of the Good; as non-being which is also a defect of goodness; and as a consequence of man's 'ignorance and difficulty'. Ignorance and difficulty were originally a natural created state of man's infancy in the struggle upwards, and therefore in no sense the result of sin, but, because of freely chosen neglect, they pass into a penal condition of blindness to the truth and of ceaseless toil. The young Augustine is emphatic that sin is in the will, not in nature. Nevertheless he allows that the goodness of a created nature can ·e diminished. Because of ignorance, 'carnal habit' has almost ᴐme nature, so that man's will, under a divine penalty, is not now free to choose the right, and indeed man has lost the power to know just what the right is (*LA* 3. 12. 36–20. 55).

## Foreknowledge and Predestination

Fourth-century Neoplatonists thought that while we have to live our lives with an uncertain future, nothing can be uncertain to God. In the third book *On Freedom of Choice* of 394, Augustine is disinclined to think divine foreknowledge causative; for if God foreknows our sins, we might then sin by necessity. If man foresees an error, his foresight does nothing to bring it about; so also with God. When in his seventies Augustine is embarrassed by the Pelagian appeal to this book, he finds it easier to discover himself teaching original sin in it than to find clear statements there about grace. He has by then come to think divine foreknowledge and predestination are identical. Even in 394 he is clear that no act of man puts God under obligations to reward him: from God all is given freely (*LA* 3. 16. 45). But once he has begun to speak of God's giving the power of the will and then the willing itself, he cannot escape linking divine foreknowledge and the preparation of the will for the assistance of grace. Grace, then, is the foundation of freedom and never the other way round. In the end Augustine comes to see that in every good action there is not one part which is ours and another that is God's: the whole belongs to both.

Step by step Augustine brings together questions about the psychology of believing (where his language is influenced by his own experience) with questions about the reasons why some are believers while others are not. About 409 he wrote for his Carthaginian friend Deogratias a little treatise (*E* 102) on objections formulated by Porphyry against the Christian faith. One is why Christianity came so late on the stage of history, and whether those either before Christ or at least outside the Biblical revelation are excluded from a salvation claimed to be universal. Augustine's comment roundly declares that God's truth may be and surely is granted to many souls throughout the world, not simply those within the orbit of Biblical religion. The truth has never been withheld from anyone anywhere who truly believes and lives a righteous life. If there remain some, however, to whom this is not granted, that is because God foreknows their refusal of his way of faith and life.

Even here, as late as 409, there is no question of divine foreknowledge being causative. The Pelagian controversy pushed him to attribute to God an active preparatory part in bringing man to faith. To him Pelagius and his friends seemed to present man as an essentially good being who, with some wise rules and commands, has the will and power to pull his socks up and to please God by holiness of life. The man Augustine sees lies in weakness and despair so profound that the only hope for him lies in an active omnipotence coming to the rescue. Assisting grace is not enough; it must also be controlling from start to finish, since if there is any point at which the will is unassisted in welcoming assistance, the final end is cast into doubt. Just as in the Donatist controversy Augustine comes to feel that the problem is insoluble without a form of coercion, so here he believes that the salvation of man cannot be achieved if there is a point at which man is left to himself. If anything can go wrong, it will.

Augustine's diagnosis of the human condition is sombre. Since Adam's fall no human being has come into the world without a perverted self-love, without an ignorance beyond that natural to childhood, and without a radically disordered emotional life. Man's love is turned away from God to the inferior and creaturely, so that he finds his love gravitating down to lust; his anger (even when justified) passing into hatred; his sadness into self-pity; even compassion at others' misfortunes (Augustine is scornful of the Stoic view that compassion is always a weakness) is easily mixed with a tiny element of horrifying satisfaction, a *Schadenfreude* which, when detected, makes one despise oneself. Accordingly, mankind is a single 'mass of sin' (*massa peccati*), one and all being equally inheritors of Adam's flawed and fallen humanity, in consequence of which the punishment of death is imposed. The irrationality and disorder of the sex instinct shows that Adam's fault is transmitted through the reproductive process. The curse of Adam and Eve is the pain and toil of raising and feeding their family. People sometimes talk, says Augustine, of the sweat and toil to which fallen Adam was condemned entirely in terms of manual labour, as if the traumas of severe intellectual work were not far more dreadful. The toil of the body is soon remedied by sleep. The toil of the mind robs one of sleep. Working with the axiom that in the world of a good and omnipotent Creator there can be no undeserved suffering, Augustine defiantly flings at Julian of Eclanum a catalogue of human agony, such as the defects of body and mind with which some are born. He asks how all this can be explained unless the race suffers under a fearful penalty for Adam's freely chosen sin. Julian lightheartedly talks as if Adam's sin merely consisted in eating an apple. From its frightful consequences must one not deduce that the 'apple' symbolizes a rebellion against God of colossal dimensions?

Because of the universal consent of humanity to sin, there is no man who, by the strictest justice, does not deserve perdition. Yet by a sovereign act of mercy God has inscrutably chosen a determinate number, indeed a substantial minority, for salvation. When St Paul says that 'God wills all to be saved' (1 Tim. 2: 4) 'all' means representatives of every race (CG 14. 44). Because his grace is truly gratis, there is no special merit in the elect to give God reasonable ground for choosing them rather than others. The divine choice is essentially antecedent to human (or angelic) merit in will, faith, and good works, all of which are also God's gift and calling.

In common with the Greek Fathers, the Pelagians base the election of God on his foreknowledge of merit. This is to make human will rather than divine grace the initiating ground of salvation, or at least that without which an initiating grace cannot be brought to its crown. Augustine on several occasions lays it down that the only thing of our very own which we contribute to our salvation is the sin from which we need to be redeemed (TJ 5. 1; S 32. 10, and elsewhere). He does not say that even redeemed man can have no merits, but rather that his merits are wholly God's gifts (E 194. 5. 19). Not that the defaced image of God has been wholly destroyed; nor that sin is ever anything but a voluntary choice. Even a person gripped fast by habit retains the bare possibility of choosing rightly. A total depravity Augustine cannot concede, or the basis of his theodicy collapses. He denies that his doctrine of predestination is one of fatalism. Its corollary is belief in final perseverance. If God gives the beginning, and if he requires moral goodness in his elect, he will ensure grace also reaches its end. Not to persevere to the end is a sign that one is reprobate. Election is therefore no ground for presumption. To persevere in holiness and righteousness all one's days is a sign that one is elect. Therefore predestination is not a ground of assurance.

Augustine's doctrine of predestination has a religious base in the Pauline doctrine of grace, but this is supported in part by philosophical arguments drawn from current Neoplatonism. The Platonists held that the cosmos, in which no event can be without a cause, is an unfolding series of emanations going back to the First Cause, the One. We inferior beings suppose ourselves to be making free choices between open possibilities but, according to the Neoplatonic schools, in the eternal knowledge of God nothing is contingent. Working with this notion Augustine has to give a special sense to free will. A human will can truly be said to be free, but it is never an originating source of action, since its role is to react to external pressure and suggestion. If it is objected that the free will of the person chosen by omnipotent grace is thenceforth in a state of necessity because it need fear no fall, Augustine is able to reply that believers (other than followers of Origen) think this anyway about the state of unfallen angels and the redeemed in heaven. Pelagianism claims that virtue and vice are what they are on the basis of an individual choice of will which is initially neutral between them. That is to claim that the absence of necessity is essential to goodness, and thereby implicitly to deny goodness to the saints in heaven, the good angels, and indeed to God himself (*OI* 5. 61).

As the controversy developed, a number of side-issues sprang into prominence. For example, sin is seen by Augustine as analogous to a debt which must somehow be paid. Christ's atonement is the 'price of the cross' which delivers man from the penalty, and in baptism that part of the debt which consists in original sin, transmitted by natural birth, is cancelled. Yet the children of baptized Christians are born sons of Adam. Moreover, concupiscence continues, for even in the baptized the flesh does not cease to lust against the spirit. Augustine therefore has some difficulty in making clear what baptism achieves.

In his studies of St Paul, one text stood out: 'What have you which you did not receive?' (1 Cor. 4: 7). If all we are by creation is God's gift to us, so much the more must that be true of redemption. To Pelagius the Creator's endowment is a possibility not to sin, aided by Biblical ethics and the moral perfection of Christ as our example. Augustine's personal experience of the divided self, acknowledging what is right but too weak in will to break out of the force of habit, convinced him that the Pelagian account is superficial. He explicitly notes that, although Julian is no heretic in Christology, Christ does not need to be more than an exceptionally wise and good man to offer the supreme model of grace and inspiration which is all that Julian speaks of (J 5. 15. 58; OI 4. 84). The true grace of Christ Augustine believes to be more inward, bringing to man's torn heart a redemptive transformation by which man comes, improbably but actually, to delight in the ethical task once so burdensome to him. How this delight may come he explains on the analogy of human love:

'Do not think you are dragged to God against your will. The mind is drawn by love which is a source of inexpressible pleasure. There is a pleasure of the heart whose sweetness consists in the bread of heaven.' Augustine quotes Virgil's second Eclogue, 'Each man's pleasure draws him on', and adds 'Give me a lover, he feels what I am talking about. Give me a man in a state of desire, of hunger, a traveller thirsty on a desert road who is sighing for the spring at his eternal home; give me a man like that, he knows what I mean. But if I address myself to a cold person, he has no notion what I am speaking of' (*TJ* 26. 4). The unutterable beauty of God is loved for itself, not for its consolations.

## A Storm of Criticism: Hell and Sex

Near the end of his life, as each successive anti-Pelagian statement became more rigid and strident, Augustine began to meet alarm and criticism from those (especially in southern Gaul, round Marseilles) who supported him in his general critique of Pelagian moralism. Was not Augustine's language about predestination of the kind that no predecessor had used? Augustine struggles to claim scripture and the support of orthodox interpreters, especially Ambrose; he observes, before citing Cyprian: 'I have not said this in a way in which no one before me has used' (*DP* 21. 55). Friends asked, Can such a doctrine of predestination be preached? Is not the preacher's appeal to his hearers' will an inherent refutation of the doctrine? Is it not offensive to tell a congregation obediently listening in church that, by eternal decree before all ages, they are already divided into sheep and goats? Is there not, in fact, force in Pelagius' original contention that the Augustinian doctrine will be destructive of morality?

The Pelagian opponents have a longer list of objections still. Julian protests at what seems to him a concept of God as ordered justice whose relentless equity to all is softened by arbitrary acts of selective mercy. The Pelagians do not dispute that baptism by water and the Spirit is necessary to gain entry to the king- dom of heaven (John 3). Yet may we not say that infants dying unbaptized, who have done no actual sin, may be admitted by God at least to an eternal life distinct from the highest joy of the kingdom, perhaps in the sense of being a natural rather than supernatural delight? Augustine asks why foundlings brought in by his nuns are baptized in time, while on occasions the babies of devoted Christian parents die before they can be baptized. But his answer to his own question is that we do not know: it is offensive in Julian to suppose that there ought to be a reason we can grasp. Julian thinks it monstrous to hold that innocent infants dying unbaptized can be consigned by a loving God to hell because of Adam's sin in eating an apple. Even Augustine grants that in their case the loss resulting from original sin will surely be extremely mild, *levissima damnatio* (*J* 5. 11. 44). In any event, Augustine protests—with a certain nobility—the natural life we are given by the order of creation is so wonderful a gift that one can never say it would be better for a man not to have existed than that he should end in separation from the company of the redeemed.

On the central problem of suffering, Augustine speaks with two voices, like a man who cannot quite make up his mind. A series of texts speaks of the miseries of this world as the consequence of sin or the punishment that sin brings with it, a punishment which divine providence can nevertheless turn to a constructive and beneficent end. He moves uneasily between the propositions that all suffering is a merited penalty for sinfulness and that all punishment decreed by God is applied by providence in such a way as to be profitable, and not merely painful and harmful. We are punished because we deserve it. But because God decrees the punishment, the experience can be for our good to teach us amendment of life. 'God never punishes an evil will to the point of annihilating the dignity of the creature ... But evil wills carry their own iniquity within them as an internal punishment' (*GL* 8. 23. 44). 'The misery under which the world groans ... is a healing pain, not a penal sentence' (*EP* 138. 15). Augustine's experience of life taught him that the punishing of delinquents often left them resentful and more antisocial afterwards than before. He asks if penalties should be strictly proportionate to the offence or if they may be modified according to the offender, since people react very differently to the same punishment. 'I do not know if any are ever corrected from falling into worse behaviour by fear of human punishment', so that one of the hardest problems facing the administration of justice in a bishop's court is to resolve the dilemma: to punish may be to ruin the man, and not to punish may be to ruin others (*E* 95. 3). If the offender is treated with hatred, the possibility of amendment is excluded (*E* 104. 3. 8).

Divine punishment is both retributive in the sense of being applied to sinners who well deserve it, and remedial. Augustine thinks it a fault in Julian's theology that, despite his insistence on free will, he has no room for hell. To take away the possibility of an ultimate refusal of admission to the presence of God is to remove the balanced perfection of a just return for final impenitence. But the divine fire is not evil, any more than the heat of the sun is made evil when it burns the criminal sentenced by the magistrates to sit in the stocks in high summer. The controversy with Julian had unhappy effects on Augustine's ideas about punishment and suffering since, if all suffering is regarded as a consequence of sin, it then begins to look prudent to avoid sin merely because of the unpleasant consequences that may ensue hereafter. Augustine elsewhere (*CR* 17. 27) stresses that the true motive for goodness is the love of God, and that to be deprived of that love by sin would be for the Christian the most formidable deterrent.

Augustine's language about hell develops in two different directions. On the one hand he becomes mountingly critical of theologians like Origen who interpret hell as psychological disintegration, and wants to insist that it is an objective reality, indeed a place 'somewhere under the earth' for both soul and body. On the other hand, he wishes to soften the doctrine and to say that there are many diversities of penalty suffered hereafter. To sin in ignorance is not excusable, but its punishment is sure to be milder than if one has acted wilfully. It is also right to believe that there may be variations and alleviations. Augustine does not much like apocryphal apostolic writings, but he feels the 'Apocalypse of Paul' may be right when it says that at Easter the souls in torment are granted rest. An important letter to Euodius (*E* 164) says he would like to think that just as at his descent to Hades the Saviour saved Adam ('as almost all Christians think'), so also he liberated good and wise men, orators, poets, and philosophers who saw polytheism to be false and were retained in the old religious tradition merely by custom—a sentence which puts us on the road to Dante.

In the 'Handbook' or *Enchiridion*, written in 421 for a high-born presbyter in Rome named Laurence, he considers the universal Christian custom of commemorating the departed. By the merit of the Mediator's sacrifice the Church rightly entreats mercy on behalf of the entire Church divided only by the narrow stream of death. The sacrifice offered in the eucharistic action gives thanks for the saints, is of no avail for the invincibly and intransigently wicked (though it may comfort surviving relations), and pleads Christ's atonement for that great number who are neither gross sinners nor perfect saints. But those who build on the foundation of faith no good works of any kind, ignoring the Ten Commandments, have not even 'wood, hay, and stubble' for the divine fire to burn away which might leave them to be 'saved but only by fire' (*FO* 16. 27–8).

Julian's most vehement onslaught is concentrated on Augustine's view of the reproductive process as the means of transmission of original sin from Adam. Here, if anywhere, he sees the cloven hoof of Manichaeism. The sexual act is a biological act which links man to the entire animal order which, by God's intention, performs it without guilt for the proper preservation of the species in each case. Sex for Julian, himself a widower, is natural and a gift of creation, 'not indeed some great good, but a physical endowment given by God'. When licit and in accord with God's commandments, the union of man and wife is exactly like that of Adam and Eve before the fall, without the least touch of anything ignoble. Julian thinks Augustine has a sombre view of the matter because of guilt he has come to feel about the foolish adolescent adventures described in the *Confessions*.

Augustine is hurt by the personal attacks but unmoved by the theological assault, confident that his estimate of sexuality is based securely on universal, and not on his own private, experience. The transmission of Adam's sin and guilt to his posterity is a proposition, he says, without which the great mass of human suffering becomes an indictment of the Creator. Sexual reproduction is the sole apparent means of transmission. Julian takes it for granted that Augustine thinks the soul is transmitted through the parental seed, and rejects this as a highly materialistic doctrine of the soul. Because he felt the force of the argument, Augustine never commits himself to this view. As a Platonist Augustine would have found the pre-existence of souls natural enough, but the psychological association of this idea with that of reincarnation barred the way there; it was also discredited by association with the dangerous speculations of Origen. He leaves open the possibility of believing that each soul is created at conception, though aware that this might seem fussy. His intransigent agnosticism concerning the origin of the soul provoked criticism to which he replied in a treatise *Concerning the Soul and its Origin* of 419–20. On this point, therefore, he escapes Julian's well-directed dart. It is not clear that he does so on the general question of the estimate of sexuality.

Augustine is convinced that sexual experience now cannot be what it was for Adam and Eve before the fall. Although the book of Genesis does not say that Adam 'knew' Eve until they were expelled from paradise, Augustine's reflection on predestination leads him to think it dangerous to suppose that Adam and Eve had no conjugal relations before the fall, and that the reproductive system was merely an afterthought of the Creator, intended to fill the gaps created by death and so to make possible the completing of the number of the elect. Augustine's argument may seem paradoxical to modern readers, but to him the argument had force: if the decree of election is prior to the fall, then sexual intercourse is so also.

Augustine's argument is drawn further and further into the realm of the speculative as he asks about the state of man before the fall. Adam and Eve, he decides, were created with the capacity to become immortal if they kept God's commandments, and would have had immortal descendants until the number of elect was complete. Their tranquil conjugal union would have been controlled not by passion but by reason and will. Eve experienced no pain—no nausea in pregnancy, no pangs in childbirth.

But of course this paradise state has gone. Now childbirth is painful. Repeatedly Augustine comes back to the observation that the physiology of sex, as now experienced, makes the capacity for union outside the mere control of the will and happens (or not) in wholly unpredictable ways, sometimes not at all when it is desired, and sometimes strongly so when the will is wholly against the act. Moreover, there is now the universal experience of shame. If Adam and Eve had not fallen, we would not feel any need to cover ourselves. Indeed there would be no tabu words for sex. (Augustine almost rests his case on the linguistic fact that some words are commonly reckoned obscene, when there is nothing in the least obscene about that to which they refer, considered objectively.) The ancient Cynics may have shown their aggressive contempt for convention by copulating in the streets, but society does not tolerate that in their fifth-century successors. The shame which leads married couples to find it natural to make love in private proves that all mankind feels there is something about sexual experience, as it now is, which belongs to the fallenness of our nature.

Surprisingly, in view of the many pages he devotes to the subject, Augustine does not find it in the least easy to say clearly, explicitly, and exactly just what this 'something' is. He is inclined to call it 'carnal concupiscence'; but this seems only to be giving a faintly pejorative description to sexual desire and to that degree begs the question to which we look for an answer. He twice says that the sexual instinct is an evil thing of which legitimate marriage makes good use (*PM* 1. 29. 57; *E* 184A. 1. 3). 'Carnal concupiscence is not sin but the daughter of sin' (*NC* 1. 24. 27), an expression of some obscurity which could easily confirm suspicion that Augustine is being deliberately oracular. Such language must in effect leave a large part of the battlefield in Julian's possession. Augustine has failed to distinguish the desire from the disorder of the affections.

Augustine is never quite consistent. Further light is thrown by his advice on the subject of married love. In ideal, he declares, sexual relations are wholly innocent if and only if their accidental pleasures are always means and never substantial ends. But he thinks it very pardonable if a husband or a wife wishes for sexual relations more than is required only by the duties of procreation. He much admires couples who live as brother and sister, and says that he knows many such who have conjugal love without intercourse (S 51. 13. 21–14. 24). The same highly ascetic sermon tells married couples wanting children that their sexual relations should be accepted 'with regret' as a necessary way of having a family. But he is well aware that the majority of married couples who love one another uniquely express their love in this way. He also raises a voice for the woman's rights. Although he regards it as a self evident truth that a woman is subordinate in the public order of society and in marriage, yet 'in mind and intelligence woman is man's equal' (C 13. 32. 47). He thinks it symbolic that Eve was made from Adam's side (CD 12. 28), suggesting a parallel role. If the wife is subordinate in marriage, this does not apply to sexual relations where her rights are equal (ME 1. 30. 63; F 22. 31). Twentieth-century man, more aware of his intimate affinity with the animal kingdom, regards sex as good and natural, but can easily make his exalted estimate of sex the concomitant of a low estimate of the institution of marriage. Augustine's relatively low view of the physical action is concomitant with a very high view of the marriage institution. Marriage is a holy thing, sanctified by Christ in the wedding at Cana. Loyalty is of the essence of the loving relation, and a man should think it a kind of 'adultery' to be discontented with his wife even if he does not go after someone else's, though society does not think in this way (*SFr* I. 12).

However exalted Augustine's claims for the marriage relation, he can turn on Julian with the certainty that St Paul reckons it better to remain unmarried for the sake of the kingdom of God. The apostle (I Corinthians 7) had granted this, in face of much more absolutist ascetics at Corinth, on the ground that an unmarried person is able to give a more wholehearted dedication to missionary activity for the Lord in the brief remaining time before the end comes. Paul also grants that married couples may properly decide to abstain for a time for the purposes of prayer. As a dedicated ascetic himself, Augustine sees sexuality, throughout his life, in the terms not so much of St Paul as of Cicero's *Hortensius*: that is, as a distraction to the soul in gaining liberation from the ties of the body. He had been 'happily married' to Adeodatus' mother, but he had not found happiness in a profounder sense, and, because of a combination of many influences, came to identify his strong sexual impulse as that which stood between him and God's love. It would be asking a lot to expect the man whose conversion to Christianity focused on a renunciation of sex to see it in the same way as Julian of Eclanum, that is as a natural gift of the good Creator to be used wholly innocently in accord with his commands.

The subsequent verdict of the Church on the controversy about grace has been to reject Pelagianism without fully endorsing the rival predestinarianism of Augustine. His extreme doctrines of predestination and perseverance long continued to provoke determined opposition in southern Gaul. Their restatement e.g. in the ninth-century Carolingian renaissance, in writers of the high middle ages like Thomas Bradwardine, by John Calvin, and then by the Jansenists of seventeenth-century France, has never failed to provoke a strong counter-reaction. Within the mainstream of traditional western Christianity, this side of Augustinianism has not been comfortably digested. At the heart of the opposition lies the conviction that Augustine never does sufficient justice to freedom. Granted that all good is the gift of divine grace, it is nevertheless an objection to Augustine that he does not leave the goodness of the people of God to be forged under trial and moral strife in the framework of this earthly life, but must anticipate the final salvation by making both it and every stage towards it independent of any instability in the creature.

A high official of the imperial administration in 414 thanked Augustine for a particularly masterful reply to a difficult question. With a polished turn of phrase he saw in its author 'everything a bishop ought to be, a philosophical mind, an informed historian, and a master of felicitous Latin' (*E* 154. 2). It could have made a fitting epitaph for him. Even during his lifetime the Latin West realized what an unrivalled master it had in this man. His misfortune was to become treated as a towering authority in the history of western Christianity in a way that he himself would have strongly deplored. A critical account of the man and of his doctrines would be a complicated and lengthy study, and the present book has been designed simply to introduce him and his ideas in the intellectual and political context of his age. There are obvious points where his arguments and standpoints invite attack, most notably his treatment of suffering, punishment, and sex. At least it may be said that Augustine himself had a deep abhorrence of being treated as a person whom people wanted to follow without pondering his reasons. He himself feared that the faith itself might suffer damage if people simply accepted his position as an authoritative statement of it. Among Early Christian theologians of comparable power only Origen is equally inclined to be so self-critical.

From time to time Augustine warns his readers about his past mistakes. In the *Confessions* the too secular tone of the Cassiciacum dialogues is subjected to a note of criticism and regret. The Pelagian controversy quickly showed that in his early writings he had not always been as exact as he would have wished. In 412 he wrote to his friend the tribune Marcellinus that he wishes to be 'one of those who write as they progress and progress as they write' (*E* 143. 2). Already in 412 he planned to publish a list of corrections to his published writings. The work envisaged appeared at last in 427 entitled 'Reconsiderations' (*Retractationes*—the Latin word does not mean 'retractions') in which he reviews ninety-three works virtually in their chronological order of composition. Usually he has something to correct or withdraw, but in many places he sets out to defend himself—the percentage proportion of withdrawal to self-defence is approximately 57 : 43. The errors he wishes to disown are either phrases open to Pelagian exploitation or Platonisms such as the depreciation of man's bodily nature or the Plotinian assumption that an unbroken mystical union with God is possible even in this life.

Let him have the last word: 'I should wish no one to embrace all my teaching except in those matters in which he has seen that I have made no mistake.... I have not followed myself in everything. I think that by God's mercy I have made progress in my writing, but not at all that I have reached perfection.... A man is of good hope if the last day of his life finds him still improving' (*DP* 21. 55).

He ends his great work *On the Trinity* with the famous prayer: 'If anything I have said comes of myself, may it be pardoned by you and by your Church.'

# SHORT READING LIST

THE standard complete edition of Augustine's works is that of the seventeenth-century Benedictines of St Maur (Paris, 1679–1700), a text reprinted in J. P. Migne's *Patrologia Latina* volumes 32–47 (Paris, 1861–2) not very accurately. Additional sermons are collected by G. Morin, *Sermones post Maurinos reperti* (Rome, 1930), and C. Lambot (Brussels, 1950). Several works are well edited in the Vienna series *Corpus Scriptorum Ecclesiasticorum Latinorum* and in the Belgian *Corpus Christianorum*.

Substantial works exist in English translation in the Oxford *Library of the Fathers* (1838–81), a series of 15 volumes edited by M. Dods, published by T. & T. Clark at Edinburgh in the 1880s. The Loeb Classical Library includes the *Confessions*, the *City of God*, and a good selection of *Letters*. A French series also gives a Latin text with translation on the facing page, *Bibliothèque Augustinienne* (39 volumes so far); this series also includes some considerable annotation. A number of works are included in English in the American series *Fathers of the Church* (CUA Press), in *Ancient Christian Writers* (Longmans), and in the *Library of Christian Classics* (SCM Press).

Biography: The best major Life of Augustine now available is by Peter Brown (Faber & Faber, 1967 and reprints), written with profound knowledge of the age and social context. See also J. J. O'Meara, *The Young Augustine* (Longmans, 1954, repr. 1980); F. van der Meer, *Augustine the Bishop* (Sheed and Ward, 1962); G. G. Willis, *St Augustine and the Donatist Controversy* (SPCK, 1950); E. Portalié, *A Guide to the Thought of St Augustine* (Burns & Oates, 1960); E. Gilson, *The Christian Philosophy of St Augustine* (Gollancz, 1961). J. Burnaby, *Amor Dei* (Hodder and Stoughton, 1938 and later reprints) remains the best study of Augustine's mystical theology. On the *City of God* see J. H. S. Burleigh, *The City of God* (Nisbet, 1949); H. A. Deane, *The Political and Social Ideas of St Augustine* (Columbia paperback, 1963). On grace and freedom see R. F. Evans, *Pelagius* (Black, 1968); Gerald Bonner, *Augustine and Modern Research on Pelagianism* (Villanova University Press, 1972); J. Patout Burns, *The Development of Augustine's Doctrine of Operative Grace* (Paris, 1980).

On the archaeological evidence for North Africa in Augustine's time there is important matter in W. H. C. Frend, *The Donatist Church* (2nd edn., Oxford 1971), though some of its theses have been disputed.


# Update 2009

Bibliography on Augustine has continued to increase. Two new collections of material have been published in the *Bibliothèque Augustinienne*: the letters discovered by Johannes Divjak in Marseilles, and the sermons discovered by François Dolbeau in Mainz. All the writings of Augustine (Latin texts with Italian translation) are now on line at <www.augustinus.it>.

The American series *Augustine for the 21st Century* (New City Press) aims to publish new annotated translations of all Augustine's writings: volumes already published include the sermons, translated by Edmund Hill, and the *Expositions of the Psalms*, translated by Maria Boulding. Among the many translations of *Confessions*, Henry Chadwick's own version (Oxford, 1991) is outstanding, and James O'Donnell's text and commentary (Oxford, 1992) is also available on-line (www.stoa.org). O'Donnell points out that Augustine was the first saint to have his own home page on the internet: see www9.georgetown.edu/faculty/jod/augustine/. *Augustine Through the Ages: An Encyclopedia* (1999), edited by Allen D. Fitzgerald OSA, is a valuable work of reference, supplemented by the Order of St Augustine website <www.augnet.org>.

The revised edition (Faber, 2000) of Peter Brown, *Augustine of Hippo*, adds two chapters on 'New Evidence' and 'New Directions'. Henry Chadwick described as 'magisterial' the work of Serge Lancel, *St Augustine* (English translation by Antonia Nevill, SCM 2002), which is helpful both on Augustine's theology and on the archaeological evidence for North Africa in his time. On *City of God,* Gerard O'Daly, *Augustine's City of God: A Reader's Guide* (OUP, 1999) is an invaluable introduction, and a revised edition of the classic study by Robert Markus, *Saeculum: History and Society in the Theology of St Augustine* (CUP) appeared in 1988.

John Rist, *Augustine: Ancient Thought Baptized* (CUP, 1994) and Carol Harrison, *Augustine: Christian Truth and Fractured Humanity* (OUP, 2000), set the central themes of Augustine's theology in the context of classical philosophy and society.

GILLIAN CLARK

# INDEX